The Criminal Investigative Function

A Guide for New Investigators

JOSEPH L. GIACALONE

Looseleaf
Law Publications, Inc.

43-08 162nd Street
Flushing, NY 11358
www.LooseleafLaw.com
800-647-5547

NOTE: All characters, stories and examples are fictional. The thoughts, feelings, stories, notes and opinions are solely that of the author and not the NYPD, John Jay College or the City of New York. This work should not be taken as legal advice and all investigators are strongly encouraged to follow their department's legal and investigative guidelines.

Library of Congress - Cataloging-in-Publication Data

Giacalone, Joseph L.
    The criminal investigative function : a guide for new investigators / Joseph L. Giacalone.
        p. cm.
    Includes bibliographical references and index.
    ISBN 978-1-60885-023-5
    1. Criminal investigation. 2. Crime scene searches.
    3. Evidence, Criminal. I. Title.
    HV8073.G5 2011
    363.25--dc22

                                                                2010047374

Cover by *Sans Serif,* Saline, Michigan

ACKNOWLEDGMENTS

I would like to give thanks to the following:

God,
My family and wife, Maria, for their support
and to Dr. Maki Haberfeld, PhD., for her
guidance and direction.

and to the Long Island Writers' Guild –
I never forgot where I came from.

*"The Journey of Criminal Investigation starts
with one giant step backwards and then
forward from there."*

— Joseph L. Giacalone

Table of Contents

About the Author

Joseph L. Giacalone is a 19-year law enforcement supervisor with an extensive background in criminal investigations. He has held many prestigious positions, but his favorite was the Commanding Officer of the Cold Case Homicide Squad. Joe has personally worked on hundreds of murders, suicides and missing person cases throughout his career and is always willing to share his knowledge and experiences with others. He is a highly decorated member of the force, including the recipient of the Medal of Valor.

He obtained a Master of Arts Degree in Criminal Justice with a Specialty in Crime and Deviance from John Jay College of Criminal Justice in 2005 and has been an Adjunct Professor at John Jay since January of 2006.

In his spare time, Joe writes his own criminal investigation Blog, http://www.ColdCaseSquad.com. Joe is a dynamic speaker and is available for training, insight, lectures, interviews and speaking engagements. He can be reached via e-mail at Joe@ColdCaseSquad.com or 516-557-9591.

You can follow Joe and the Cold Case Squad Blog on www.twitter.com/coldcasesquad

Introduction

Why did I write this book? With all of the criminal investigation textbooks out there, you are probably wondering, "Isn't one text just as good as or better than the next?" The answer to that question is no. Over the past few years I have used and adopted a variety of textbooks from different companies and authors and I was never happy with any of them in particular. In addition, most academic textbooks are still patrol officer centric and not in tune with the criminal investigative function. For instance, pick up a textbook on criminal investigation and turn to the 8 Major Felonies. They are more concerned with responding to the scene then with the actual criminal investigation. The investigator's role is a reactionary one and do not respond to in-progress crimes.

My biggest concern was that many of the texts used today in police academies, colleges and universities across the country were written by authors, who were never police officers, let alone ever been to a crime scene. This is not an academic textbook; it was written by a practitioner.

This book was written almost entirely from my experiences, my mistakes, what I learned and what I know. I've held the position of Investigator, Executive Officer of a Detective Squad and the Commanding Officer of a Cold Case Homicide Squad. In addition to my field assignments, for three years I was the Director of the Department's Homicide School. I hold a Master of Arts Degree in Criminal Justice with a Specialty in Crime and Deviance and I have been an adjunct professor for the past four years.

I'm glad you have interest in the field of law enforcement and more specifically criminal investigation. Even though all law enforcement agents conduct some aspect of criminal investigation, most are involved only in a limited role known as the preliminary investigation. This text was written for the Criminal Justice Student and for the training of new investigators. Today's investigators have to be computer savvy, great communicators, have a strong understanding of physical evidence and be undaunted by politics from inside as well as outside of their department. This text will prepare the groundwork for your new career. It will teach you the necessary investigative techniques, but only through practical experience will you ever master them.

I also gave this text a different kind of look. The book is broken down as if it were a real investigation. You are the investigator sitting at your desk typing a report when the phone rings. From the time the case comes across your desk to the time you'd testify in the courtroom and everything in between is covered. Anytime throughout the text that you see the word "you" I mean investigator. I wanted you to learn about criminal investigation, not just by learning concepts, but with a little infusion of humor and a number of acronyms that allow the student the opportunity to memorize and never forget. I wanted the reader to feel the investigative experience as best as they could through words by inspiring their imagination. It's easy reading because it's in plain English: no legal mumbo jumbo or scientist "speak."

After each chapter, there are a number of "Questions for Discussion and Review," that are designed not only to be thought provoking, but to drill the concepts into your head. Give them a try, they're definitely not going to hurt you. I am not going to waste your time with information that you don't need to know, or fill the pages with fluff that prolong the issue. This book was written to give the student investigator what they need to know and go out and do the job.

Good luck with your chosen path. It is most rewarding!

— Joseph L. Giacalone

Chapter 1

The Criminal Investigative Process

"These detective shows on TV always end at precisely the right moment—after the criminal is arrested and before the courts turns him loose."
— Robert Orben

How does one become an investigator? This is probably the most asked question in Criminal Justice classrooms all around the world. I know it is asked in my classes quite often. The investigator position is probably the most sought after position in any police department and is usually bestowed on those that are most worthy. Television has done even more to glorify the investigative position with the myriad of shows surrounding the topic.

It all starts off with taking a civil service examine to become a sworn uniformed patrol officer. No one walks out of the academy and into a "suit." During years of patrol service, some officers develop the potential of becoming a good investigator by their quality of work, street smarts, experiences and apprehension record. Eventually, all of these activities get noticed by the higher ups within the department. A careful selection process is not only based on merit, but officer behavior is also taken into consideration. Because the investigator position has a certain level of autonomy coupled with the fact that they wear "regular" or "soft" clothes, officers must have an exceptional background.

Schedules for investigators can be unpredictable at times. Investigators may be required to work at odd hours depending on current crime patterns/trends and sometimes work all day and night when heavy cases (murder, rape, shooting, terrorism) cross their desk. The investigator position is not as neat, clean and "sexy" as it is portrayed on television cop shows and could make family life difficult at times. All police work is tough on family life, period.

Many police departments, if not all, dole out their investigator positions as an "investigative track" and not through an exam. An investigative track exists to ensure that

1

the very best street cops are chosen to eventually become investigators. A track may consist of the following steps: Patrol Officer ➤ Plain Clothes Officer ➤ Investigator. The patrol assignment develops the officer's skills at conducting preliminary investigations and the plain clothes assignment develops their apprehension abilities.

The sought after "gold shield" is not presented to the officer after a plain clothes assignment, but after they continue the investigative track in the Investigations Bureau of the department for an additional eighteen (18) months. From the time you enter the police academy to the end of the 18-month track within the Investigations Bureau, it could take an individual as long as ten (10) years! Students who want to do this for their future law enforcement career must be mentally prepared for the long road ahead of them.

The investigator, like other police tasks, does more than just investigate cases. The victim/family advocate is a role that is often left off the list of investigator job functions. Investigators represent the victim when he/she is no longer capable of doing it themselves and most importantly they provide closure to families that allow the healing processes to begin. Out of the many roles that I maintained in the police force, it was the most satisfying and rewarding.

Qualities of an Investigator

The qualities of an effective investigator run the gamut. But the most important qualities are to be a **PD COP**:

Persistent
Determined

Communicator
Oriented toward details
Prepared

- **Persistent**

The investigator will have to overcome many obstacles during the course of an entire case. For example, there can be a lack of evidence, frustration with eyewitnesses, missed apprehension opportunities, a series of crimes committed by one perpetrator with no leads in sight, inquisitive media representatives, demanding district attorneys and most frustrating, answering questions about the case to "Down-town." How persistent do you have to be? Like a pit bull, you clamp down on something and don't let go until the facts and evidence prove otherwise.

• Determined

After dealing with the frustration and disappointment that often occurs in cases, the investigator has to press on and keep digging for new clues, information and leads that can help solve the case. It may require re-interviewing people, reviewing evidence logs and crime scene photos, conducting follow up conferrals with the police laboratory, other enforcement agencies and the district attorney. The investigator must remain focused and objective throughout the course of the investigation and subsequent trial.

• Communicator

The majority of the time an investigator spends on the case will be talking to people: victims, witnesses or anyone that can help. The investigator must have the skill to extract information from people, especially those unwilling to provide information to the police, especially when he is wearing a t-shirt that says, "Stitches 4 Snitches." Say the wrong word, or show bad non-verbal body language and the information can be gone forever. Can you imagine knocking on someone's door at 3 o'clock in the morning and asking them to help you?

• Oriented toward details

It's the little things that solve crimes, like great observation skills. Examples: Were the lights on or off? Was anything obviously moved? Is there something present at the scene that shouldn't be? The trace evidence recovered after a careful search of a crime scene, or asking the right question to the right person can mean the difference in solving or not solving the case. If the investigator takes shortcuts, gets lazy, or does not prioritize investigative leads then the case will end up cold. The details of the investigation must also be documented carefully. A failure to document could allow a guilty person to walk free. If it was not documented on a report, it is considered never done.

- **Prepared**

The investigator has to be "up" on the case because he/she never knows when they are going to get the break they need. As you will learn in a Chapter 6, an interrogation will not take place until all information that is available is obtained. The investigative reports must be typed, submitted in a timely fashion and kept neat in the case folder. Proper indexing (Figure 1.1) of reports makes it easier to read and retrieve information, especially in the courtroom years later. An investigator never knows when or if the case will garner media attention and therefore Downtown's attention.

Figure 1.1

Case # _____   Complaint # _____

Report #	Date	Description	Observations Day	From	To
1	1/1/2009	Notification of Incident			
2	1/1/2009	Response to the Scene			
3	1/1/2009	Canvass of 123 ABC Street			
4	1/1/2009	Receipt of Victim's Property			
5	1/1/2009	Canvass for Surveillance Video			
6	1/1/2009	Suspect Still Created from Surveillance Video			
7	1/1/2009	Subpoena for Cell Phone Information			
8	1/3/2009	Crime Stoppers Tip regarding Surveillance Still			
9	1/3/2009	Computer Checks on Johnny Jones			
10	1/3/2009	DMV request for Photograph			
11	1/7/2009	Photo Array Shown to Witness			
12	1/8/2009	Observation at the home of Johnny Jones	Friday	1600	2000
13	1/9/2009	Receipt of Photos from Surveillance			
14	1/10/2009	Arrest of Suspect Johnny Jones			

The index in Figure 1.1 is short, but you should under-stand how important it is. It provides an investigative frame-work for what has been done and what should be done. An index can also allow the investigator to find a specific report. Can you imagine looking through a case folder of 150 to 200 reports without an index? The defense lawyer will label you and your investigation sloppy and disorganized.

What is Criminal Investigation?

What is criminal investigation? Criminal investigation contains the **CORE** elements to determine what happened, why it happened and who did it. Criminal investigation is the process by which an investigator:

Collects
Organizes
Records
Evaluates evidence and information

An investigator completes these tasks with the thought in mind of someday testifying at trial. An investigation does not end with the arrest, but with the successful prosecution of the case. An investigator must follow a case through until the perpetrator that was responsible is apprehended, tried, convicted and shipped off to corrections.

Goals of Investigation

The goals of investigation are to make sure the case does not go **DOA**:

Determine whether a crime was committed
Obtain information and evidence to identify perpetrators
Arrest suspects and present the case to the prosecutor

- **Determine whether a crime was committed**

There are only two (2) categories of crimes: (1) Misde-meanors and (2) Felonies. The definition of a crime does not include violations and traffic infractions. The student must be aware that each public enterprise, whether it is the local, state or federal government, has different names, definitions and penalties for crimes. However, the following information generally applies to most jurisdictions: misdemeanors are considered minor crimes and felonies are more serious. Therefore, penalties are handed down accordingly. If convicted of a misdemeanor, an individual can be punished by a fine and/or imprisoned for a term not to exceed one year. The individual will serve their time in a local jail. If convicted of a felony, an individual can be sentenced to over one (1) year in jail—a year and a day plus in a state penitentiary. The student now knows that the next time they read the newspaper and see, "Johnny Jones was arrested for a crime," they know he committed a felony or a misdemeanor. Allegedly of course!

> **CI Tip Sheet**
> Misdemeanor = small crime, small time, small jail
> Felony = big crime, big time, "the big house"

Violations, traffic infractions and civil matters would not rise to the level of a crime (misdemeanor or felony) in most instances; therefore they would not be treated in the same manner.

- **Obtain information and evidence to identify perpetrators**

The investigator searches for trace evidence, body fluids, fingerprints, ballistics and other physical evidence so that these unknown samples can be matched up against known databases: Combined DNA Index System (CODIS), the Integrated Automatic Fingerprint Identification System (IAFIS), Integrated Ballistic Identification System (IBIS), etc.

In addition, victim and witness statements and identification procedures such as a show up, arrays, and lineups, play a pivotal role in identifying perpetrators (Chapter 5). Investigators spend a tremendous amount of time communicating with people to develop information. Sometimes, statements given by suspects provide crucial evidence in cases. Also, both public and private computer databases provide information regarding people (victim, witness, and perpetrator), places (location of occurrence) and things (vehicles, firearms, etc.).

- **Arrest suspects and present the case to the prosecutor**

The ultimate goal is to tie a suspect to a crime based on evidence and witness/victim statements. Criminal investigation is not a solo "sport," but requires a team of highly trained and experienced investigators. There is no "I" in Team, but there is an M and an E. An investigator must be careful and not let their ego spoil an investigation.

In order for the police to make an arrest, they must follow specific guidelines. Remember, arresting someone is a "seizure" and the law enforcement community must be mindful of the U.S. Constitution and the rights protected under the 4th Amendment. In essence, court decisions and legislation have carved out three (3) exceptions to obtaining an arrest warrant. Police officers must remember their **CAPS** before leaving the stationhouse.

Committed in the officer's presence
Arrest Warrant
Probable Cause
Statutory

- **Committed in the officer's presence**

If a crime or a violation occurs in the officer's presence, he/she can make an arrest without obtaining a warrant. This is also known as a "pick up arrest." For example, the police officer is driving by in his car and sees a teenager grab a lady's pocketbook and run. He can chase him down and arrest him. Can you imagine telling the perpetrator, "You wait here while I get an arrest warrant. I'll be back in a few hours to arrest you."

- **Arrest Warrant**

If you read the 4th Amendment in the strictest possible sense, no one would ever be arrested unless a warrant was issued (see example in Committed in the Officer's Presence).

An arrest warrant is signed by a judge after the officer presents a written affidavit showing satisfactory Probable Cause (see below). The warrant will state the name of the individual to be seized and a demand to bring them to court to answer to the charge. Arrest warrants are executable any time of the day and any day of the week. They include weekends and holidays!

An investigator has to be aware of one caveat in regards to obtaining an arrest warrant—it also comes with an absolute right to counsel. In the event that the perpetrator is apprehended, the police cannot interrogate him unless his/her lawyer is present. There is no chance of ever obtaining a confession or admission from the perpetrator (Chapter 6). But sometimes you have no choice. For example, if your perpetrator is located in another state, they can detain him as "For Other Authorities (FOA)," but you have to obtain an arrest warrant to extradite him back to your jurisdiction.

- **Police Standards of Proof (Levels of Suspicion)**

There are only four (4) levels of suspicion that dictate police/citizen encounters. At each level the police have different powers granted to them. The student must understand that a police stop could amount to a seizure, which would be protected under the 4th Amendment. It all hinges on the level of freedom that is taken away.

CI Tip Sheet

A police officer needs Probable Cause for three (3) things:
   (1) To make an arrest
   (2) To obtain an arrest warrant
   (3) To obtain a search warrant.

Here are the four (4) Levels of Suspicion, also known as Standards of Proof, in order from least to most:

Standard 1 - Request for Information

A Request for Information is the lowest level of suspicion. If the police have any suspicion, they can approach anyone for an articulable reason, to inquire, and to ask them what they are doing or other general questions. The individual does not have to answer, which is protected under the 5th Amendment. At this level of suspicion the police cannot forcibly stop the individual or detain them in anyway. (*People v. DeBour* 40 NY 2d. 210 (1976)).

Standard 2 - Mere Suspicion

Mere Suspicion is defined as a hunch or gut feeling the officer has that criminal activity may or did take place. At this level of suspicion the police cannot make a forcible stop, but can keep them under surveillance or they can walk up to the individual and ask them pointed questions under the common law writ of inquiry (*People v. DeBour* 40 NY 2d. 210 (1976)). Based on the persons answers and actions, the police may develop enough information to rise to the next standard, Reasonable Suspicion.

Standard 3 - Reasonable Suspicion

Observations made by a police officer that would come to the reasonable conclusion that a person is committing has committed or is about to commit a felony or penal law misdemeanor. At this level of suspicion the police can stop, question and (possibly) frisk. More on reasonable suspicion and the "Terry Stop" can be found in Chapter 4, "Exceptions to a Search Warrant (*Terry v. Ohio* 392 U.S. 1 (1968))."

Standard 4 - Probable Cause

The term Probable Cause comes directly from the 4th Amendment. It is the standard of proof that is required to make an arrest and obtain both an arrest warrant and a search warrant. "Probable cause exists when evidence or information which appears reliable discloses facts or circumstances which are collectively of such weight and persuasiveness as to convince a person of ordinary intelligence, judgment and experience that it is reasonably likely that such offense was committed and that such person committed it (New York State Criminal Procedural Law Section 70.10)." In simpler terms, the evidence points to the fact that a crime was committed and the person arrested committed it.

Statutory

An officer cannot make an arrest for violations not in their presence. For example, a slap to the face leaving no injuries is a violation known as Harassment in most jurisdictions. If this "slap" is not witnessed by the officer, no arrest can be made. Now you may ask yourself, "What's the big deal, there are no injuries." But, what if the case involves a domestic violence (DV) incident? Over the past decade or so, legislators have drafted statutes to provide the police with more discretion regarding making an arrest for violations in DV cases.

A police officer has the final say if an arrest is made even if the injured party does not want an arrest. Once the police feel that the peace will not continue after they leave, an arrest will be made. "Someone is going": police slang for making an arrest.

Functions of Evidence

The investigator will sift through and identify many types of evidence that serve different functions during the course of an investigation. An investigator may have little evidence or many types. Evidence can be either inculpatory, which is evidence that shows involvement and tends to establish guilt, or exculpatory, evidence that can exonerate by eliminating them from contention.

The law enforcement community has an obligation to hand over all of the evidence, especially exculpatory evidence, discovered during the course of an investigation to the suspect's defense, even if it means putting the case at risk. The U.S. Supreme Court decided in *Brady v. Maryland* 373 U.S. 83 (1963) that prosecutors must disclose all exculpatory evidence. If they don't, they violate the suspect's due process rights covered under the 14th Amendment. On a recent case in San Francisco on June 23, 2009, *Tennison v. San Francisco*,

No. 06-15426, the appeals court applied *Brady v. Maryland* to the police. The police are mandated to disclose all exculpatory evidence.

CI Tip Sheet

INculpatory Evidence = **IN**cludes
EXculpatory = **EX**cludes or **EX**onerates

Depending on the type of evidence, it would be wise for an investigator to make an appointment with **DR. C**orpus **CAB**.

Direct
Real

Corpus Delicti

Circumstantial
Associative
Behavioral

- **Direct Evidence**

Is any evidence that demonstrates an existence of a fact. No inferences or presumptions are necessary with direct evidence. Examples of direct evidence are an eyewitness's testimonial account, video surveillance, statements made by witnesses, victims and the perpetrator. A victim points to her bruise and states, "My husband punched me in the eye," or a bank video camera taking pictures of the individual robbing the bank are examples of direct evidence. Direct evidence is the opposite of indirect or circumstantial evidence.

- **Real Evidence**

Real evidence is also known as Physical Evidence. Physical Evidence is anything that has real properties, can be touched, seen, and collected as the result of a criminal act. For example, a person was bludgeoned to death with a heavy object and blood splatter can be seen on the walls and ceiling. The blood splatter is real (physical) evidence. Other important examples of real evidence are: biological fluids, fibers, bite marks, ballistic, soil, tool marks, teeth impressions, shoe impressions, fingerprints, etc.

- ### Corpus Delicti Evidence

Latin for "body of the crime," is evidence that establishes that a crime actually occurred. For example, the police respond to a location and find a woman with multiple stab wounds in the back. For the investigators, suicide would seem unlikely. This would be corpus delicti evidence that a murder occurred. The term corpus delicti does not mean the body itself! Remember, the medical examiner is the only person than can classify the manner of death as a homicide.

- ### Circumstantial Evidence

Circumstantial evidence, also known as Indirect Evidence, is evidence that makes an inference that a person is responsible for a crime. The USlaw.com website defines Circumstantial Evidence as, "a collection of facts that, when considered together, can be used to infer a conclusion about something unknown." For example, the police execute a search warrant on the home of a man whose girlfriend was found shot to death. During the search the police recover the firearm. Believe it or not, the firearm is physical evidence, but still circumstantial—it could have been put there by someone else, unlikely, but remember the prosecution has the burden of proof. Ballistics will tell us if the gun was the one used in the murder. However, further investigative methods might prove it to be direct evidence by recovering fingerprints off of the gun or bullets, identifying gunshot residue from the boyfriend's hand or clothes or a witness statement saying she saw him with the gun in the hallway. In rare cases, circumstantial evidence alone may be used to convict someone. However, in most cases, an investigator identifies direct evidence to corroborate the circumstantial evidence.

- **Associative Evidence**

Associative evidence establishes linkage between suspects and victims, suspects with crime scenes, a tool with tool marks, etc. Associative evidence is closely tied into the Locard's Exchange Principle. Anyone that has a dog or cat is well aware of associate evidence. Just look at your pants!

- **Behavioral Evidence**

Behavioral evidence has to do with the psychological state of the offender and is used to build a profile. The basics of behavioral evidence are the Modus Operandi (MO) and the Signature. The MO is the "method of operation" that the crime was committed and the signature is the part of the crime that provides emotional satisfaction to the perpetrator (Turvey, 2008, p 198). Think of MO and signature in this analogy: The MO is the restaurant you prefer, signature is the type of food you eat in that restaurant.

The Investigation Flow Chart

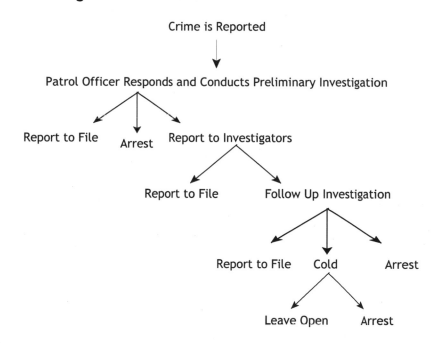

A criminal investigation is broken down into two (2) main parts:

(1) the Preliminary Investigation and
(2) the Follow Up Investigation.

In this section we are going to tackle the preliminary investigation.

After a crime is reported, radio communications will dispatch the call for assistance to a uniformed patrol officer. The patrol officer responds to and begins the preliminary investigation at the scene. The first responsibility of the responding officer is to protect life. Even if the bad guy is climbing out of the window when they arrive, their first priority is to the injured person. In that case it would be perfectly acceptable to broadcast a description of the perpetrator and a direction of flight. If necessary, patrol officers will detain witnesses, establish a crime scene and make notifications.

The preliminary investigation is a brief probing for facts and to identify evidence. In some cases it includes the arrest of the perpetrator. If no crime was committed, or if it was a civil matter, the officer will take the report, make referrals if necessary, close the case and file the report with the stationhouse clerk. The report must have the most number of facts and follow a logical approach to solvability. The officer will attempt to answer the following six (6) basic questions: When, Where, Who, What, How and Why.

If the report has at least one (1) solvability factor, such as the nature of the crime (felony), named perpetrator, physical evidence, eyewitness, or biological evidence, the officer will leave the case open and refer it to an investigator. In cases of murder, rape, shootings/stabbings and pattern crime cases that referral and notification will be made directly from the scene whenever possible.

A thorough preliminary investigation and a prompt notification to an investigator are the keys to solving and clearing cases.

Questions for Discussion and Review:

1. Who is responsible to conduct the preliminary investigation? _____

2. In your opinion, when would be a good time to execute an arrest warrant?

3. Is it true that circumstantial evidence is not admissible in court? Explain

4. Real evidence is also known as? _____

5. What are the three (3) exceptions to obtaining an arrest warrant?

6. Why is it so important for the police to determine if a crime was even committed before moving forward?

7. If convicted of a felony, how long can you be sentenced to? _____

8. Should the patrol officer have a more expanded role in the overall investigation? Why or why not?

9. What is the difference between circumstantial evidence and direct evidence?

10. The level of suspicion that a police officer must have before making an arrest is? _____

11. Provide two (2) examples of inculpatory and exculpatory evidence.

12. Would the theft of a car spark an immediate investigation? Why or why not?

13. Can the police arrest a dead person? Why or why not?

14. In order to make an arrest, the police must always have an arrest warrant. True/False

15. Opinion: What day of the year would be a good one to look for a suspect that has been on the run?

Chapter 2

Criminal Identification Systems

"One can only see what one observes and one observes only things which are already in the mind."
— Alphonse Bertillon

Over the last 125 years and counting, progress has been made on ways the police identify individuals who are responsible for committing crimes. As the means of identifying criminals developed, new technologies surfaced and proved more useful and reliable than their predecessors. These identification systems are extremely important in ensuring that the police apprehend the right person. Not only can these systems be used to convict a guilty person, but they can also exonerate an innocent person. It should be known however, that generally an identification of an individual through one of these systems will not be the sole factor in determining guilt or innocence. It will be used by the prosecution in conjunction with other factors such as: physical evidence, victim statements, eyewitness identification, statements made, etc.

Recently, investigators and prosecutors have been handed a set back in single eyewitness identification cases in *People v. LeGrand* 8 N.Y.3d 449 (2007). This case allows the use of experts in the field of misidentification to present the problems of eyewitness identification to the jury. More than ever, investigators must painstakingly search for and identify physical evidence instead of relying on a single eyewitness.

There are (were) three (3) major systems of criminal identification that have been developed over the years. Investigators must take their time processing crime scenes so evidence can **ADD** up.

Anthropometry
Dactylography
Deoxyribonucleic Acid

Anthropometry (Body Measurements)

Anthropometry, or body measurements, was developed by Alphonse Bertillon. Bertillon believed that taking and recording measurements of the skeletal system was an accurate means of identifying criminals. Bertillon calculated that there was a 270 million to-one chance that two people could have fourteen identical measurements (height, length and width of head, length of left forearm, etc.) He felt that anthropometry would be accurate identifier because once a person reaches a certain age the bone structure will remain the same. (NYC.gov).

The Bertillon method of identifying criminals was used for about twenty years before it was replaced by Dactylography (fingerprinting). Alphonse Bertillon was the vanguard on criminal identification as well as criminal photographs. For his foresight and devotion to the topic, Bertillon has become known as the "Father of Criminal Identification."

Dactylography (Fingerprints)

Dactylography, better know as fingerprinting, was first suggested in the late 1880s as a means of identifying criminals by Dr. Henry Fauld. Even though fingerprinting had early successes, it was not adopted for over two decades, when it officially replaced Anthropometry as the standard in identifying criminals.

Other contributors to the identification of criminals with fingerprints are:

- Francis Galton - wrote the seminal book, *Finger Prints* - which had a set of his own prints on the cover
  - Established three distinct fingerprint patterns: Loops, Whorls and Arches
    - Arches are the rarest fingerprint pattern

- Edward Henry - established the classification system to file fingerprints, known as the Henry System, which is still used today throughout the world

Fingerprints are formed by the mixture of perspiration, dirt and the oil from our skin. There are three types of fingerprints that can be found at a crime scene that can lead us to our **VIP**:

Visible
Invisible
Plastic

- **Visible**

Visible prints, also known as Patent prints can be seen with the naked eye and requires no other process to make them visible. They can be found in blood, paint or any type of thick liquid.

- **Invisible**

A Latent, or invisible a print that is invisible to the naked eye, requires another process, like dusting or an alternative light source, to make them visible. The light source can be from a simple flashlight. Once it is visible, the investigator will ensure that it is photographed, without and with a ruler) before any attempt is made to lift it. This is done in case the print gets destroyed during the lifting process.

CI Tip Sheet

The proper order to secure fingerprint evidence is to:
Dust
Photograph
Lift

- **Plastic**

Plastic prints are also visible to the naked eye and can be formed in clay, tape, gum, or glue. Patent and plastic prints will also be photographed in the same manner as latent prints, but the investigator should make an effort to see if they can take the entire object with them. Today, the system of filing fingerprints has become an electronic forensic database called the Integrated Automated Fingerprint Identification System (IAFIS - pronounced: Eye-A-Fiss) which is maintained by the FBI. Each state has their own database called AFIS which is linked to the FBI's IAFIS database. An unknown set of prints are loaded into the system and run against the known database. IAFIS and AFIS contain prints not only from criminals, but everyday citizens who have already been fingerprinted for a license, job, passport, etc.

AFIS can be helpful in identifying **LSD**:

- **L**iars
- **S**uspects
- **D**eceased and missing persons

If the computer database gets a "hit (match)," then a fingerprint technician will retrieve the prints for the file and make a physical inspection by eye, magnifying glass and microscope. Then another technician will conduct similar tests to back up the AFIS hit and the human match. The human element is never eliminated because a computer says it's a match.

Deoxyribonucleic Acid (DNA)

Deoxyribonucleic Acid or DNA for short, is the genetic blueprint that determines everything from our hair color to our disease vulnerabilities. The DNA "fingerprint" was discovered in 1984 England by Dr. Sir Alec Jeffreys who determined that each person has a unique DNA makeup, with the exception of identical twins.

In the village of Enderby England, 1988, DNA quickly became a reliable method of identifying individuals when Dr. Jeffreys's technique combined with old fashioned police work, was used to exonerate one suspect and identify another, Mr. Colin Pitchfork, for the rape and murder of two young women (Connors, Lundregan, Miller & McEwen, 1996, p.4). Known as the Enderby Case, this was the seminal point that ushered in a new era for criminal investigation.

There are two (2) types of DNA, (1) Nuclear DNA (cell has a nucleus) and (2) Mitochondrial DNA (mtDNA) (cell has no nucleus). Nuclear DNA is derived from both parents and mtDNA is only derived from the mother. Every cell, tissue, organ, etc. in our bodies has the same DNA. A hair follicle has nuclear DNA in the bulb, but not in the shaft. A shaft of hair recovered at a crime scene will have testing limitations due to the fact that it only contains mtDNA. There is a greater chance of finding mtDNA than nuclear DNA because it contains hundreds of copies of the genome as compare to only two (2) found in the nucleus (The DNA Initiative, DNA.gov). MtDNA can also be found in fingernail scrapings and teeth. Nuclear DNA can be found in all of the following: White blood cells, tooth pulp, spermatozoa, bone marrow, hair roots, saliva, cheek cells (buccal—pronounced "buckle"—cells), sweat and skin cells. Nuclear DNA is not found in red blood cells.

Mitochondrial DNA played a big role in identifying victims of the World Trade Center. Some pieces that were recovered were the size of a quarter, but through the use of mtDNA, they could be positively identified. In order to get a match of mtDNA, the investigator found a donor derived from the mother: a victim's brother, sister, maternal grandmother, and had it compared against a local DNA database. Some victims were identified years later after their remains were recovered during the cleanup and new construction. Because of the scientific advancements and the use of mtDNA during the identification process of the WTC, mtDNA has become a court accepted method of identifying people.

CI Tip Sheet

Mitochondrial is derived from Mom

The main database run by the FBI is called CODIS or the Combined DNA Index System. CODIS allows federal, state and local crime laboratories to exchange and share DNA profiles electronically (NIJ, Issue 249, 2003). CODIS is comprised of two (2) databases: The Forensic and the Offender Database. The Forensic (Unknown) Database includes DNA profiles from unknown individuals that where recovered from crime scenes. The Offender (Known) Database contains the DNA profiles of individuals who were convicted of certain crimes. Each state has different statutes that trigger taking a sample from a convict. DNA found at a crime scene is uploaded into CODIS in the hopes of identifying a known subject. CODIS is to DNA as IAFIS is to fingerprints and IBIS is to ballistics.

What happens if we (investigators) have obtained DNA evidence at a crime scene and we really "like" a particular individual for the crime? How can the investigator legally obtain a DNA Exemplar from the "suspect?" An investigator can obtain a DNA sample legally from an individual by using the three **C**s:

(1) **C**onsent
(2) **C**ourt Order
(3) **C**overtly

For example, a woman is brutally stabbed to death in her home. There are no signs of a forced entry or of a struggle. The victim was found in the back bedroom, fully clothed. The investigators suspect the ex-boyfriend who was observed on the block at the time of the incident. Fingernail scrapings from the victim were taken and a profile of a male donor was able to be extracted. However, the profile does not match any profile in CODIS.

In the above event, the only viable way to obtain a DNA sample from the ex-boyfriend would be to do it covertly. You do not have probable cause to obtain a warrant and if you ask for consent, you may frighten him away. So obtaining a sample covertly is your only viable option. You can accomplish this by following the individual and waiting for them to spit, drop a cigarette or chewing gum, or he can be brought in to "help" with the investigation and an attempt would be made to secure an abandonment sample. It could be in the form of a tissue, chewing gum, can of soda or bottle of water. The exemplar would be collected, packaged, and submitted for DNA testing against the unknown sample from the crime scene.

What is a DNA Exemplar? An exemplar is an example from individuals who may/may not have anything to do with the crime. For instance, fingerprints are found at the scene of a murder inside of a home. The police would take exemplars, or elimination samples, in this case fingerprints, from all individuals who had lawful access to the location. Elimination prints will be compared to the prints found at the scene, instead of uploading them into AFIS. This saves both time and money. There are four types of exemplars that the police can encounter during an investigation.

The investigator must **SAVE** the following:

Suspect sample
Abandonment sample
Victim sample
Elimination sample

Admissibility of DNA Evidence

Advances in DNA typing appear to be limitless. No one knows for sure how far or how fast DNA typing will develop in identifying criminal suspects. But what we do know is that it is very reliable. The question is will the new scientific techniques be admissible in court? and if not how long will it take? When DNA is introduced as evidence at a trial, an expert (forensic scientist, criminalist, etc.) will testify about what examinations were done and how they were done. This testimony will be affected by two (2) court decisions, depending on what state you live in: The Frye Standard and the Daubert Standard.

The Frye Standard (*Frye v. United States* 293 F. 1013 (1923)) states that in order for a scientific technique to be admissible, the technique must be sufficiently established to have gained general acceptance in its particular field to which it belongs. The Frye Standard is tougher to prove because some new methods have not been accepted yet.

In *Daubert v. Merrell Dow Pharmaceuticals, Inc.* 507 US 904 (1993), the Supreme stated that the trial judge will make an independent assessment of expert reliability as well as the processes and procedures used in a pre-trial hearing. The Supreme Court was trying to limit the amount of courtroom showdowns between experts. The Daubert decision applies only to cases within the federal court, but this standard has been adopted by several states.

Questions for Discussion and Review:

1. Which season of the year are investigators most likely to obtain fingerprints at a crime scene? Why?

2. What are the three (3) ways that the police can legally obtain a DNA exemplar?

3. Should everyone at birth be required to submit a DNA sample for the CODIS database? Why or why not?

4. In your opinion, which system of identification, DNA or fingerprints, is more reliable and why?

5. How many chromosomes does the average human have? Is there any difference between men and women's chromosomes? Animals?

6. What are the four (4) types of DNA exemplars discussed in this chapter?

7. Why are buccal cells (cheek cells) an excellent location to retrieve nuclear DNA?

8. Which parent is mtDNA derived from?

9. Which standard, Frye or Daubert is the toughest on the Criminal Justice System and why?

10. Which crime(s) do you think that DNA can be used to exonerate the innocent as well as convict the guilty?

11. What are the three (3) types of fingerprint types discussed in this chapter?

12. Which standard, Frye of Daubert, does your state follow?

Chapter 3

Search and Seizure

"The police must obey the law while enforcing the law."
— Chief Justice Earl Warren

What is Search and Seizure? A search, as the term suggests, is a methodical and purposeful activity that looks to secure evidence that will be used to prosecute the perpetrator. A Seizure is the confiscation of evidence, goods or persons found during a search for the purpose of securing it and using it against the perpetrator in a court of law.

Investigators know that during the course of an investigation many constitutional issues come into play. They must be careful not to infringe on anyone's rights or risk being sued and losing the case. There are two important court cases that provide the history behind search and seizure and law enforcement. The student must understand "where we were" in order to get a grasp of "how we got here." Next to custodial interrogation, the topic of search and seizure is a highly contested subject amongst civil libertarians and crime control advocates.

I am only providing you a basic outline of what occurred in these cases; they are more involved that what I wrote. The student is encouraged to research these cases in depth. Here is any easy way to research a Supreme Court decision: For example, take a look at the following fictitious citation:

P   D
Smith v. Jones - 123 U.S. 456 2010

- Smith is the **P**laintiff
- Jones is the **D**efendant
- 123 would be the volume number of the law report the decision was published
- U.S. - United States Report
- 456 is the page number in volume 123 where the information can be obtained
- 2010 is the year in which the decision was rendered

Here are the search and seizure cases that you should be familiar with:

1. *Weeks v. The United States* - 232 U.S. 383 (1914)

Quick Case Synopsis:

Freemont Weeks of Kansas City Missouri, was accused of sending lottery tickets through the mail, a federal crime. Federal agents entered Weeks' home and seized papers and other evidence against him. Later on that same day, more federal agents entered his home and retrieved more evidence. Both times the agents did not posses a warrant. The evidence was subsequently used to convict him of the crime.

Results of the Case:

- The U.S. Supreme Court overturns Weeks' conviction by a unanimous decision (9-0) citing a violation of the 4th Amendment
- The decision gave birth to the Federal Exclusionary Rule
  - o   Any evidence obtained in violation of the 4th Amendment will be inadmissible in Federal Court
- This led to the "Silver Platter Doctrine" - The Federal Exclusionary Rule did not prevent state officials from handing over evidence obtained in violation of the 4th Amendment to federal agents on a "Silver Platter."

Famous quote from the case: Justice William Rufus Day

"If letters and private documents can thus be seized and held and used in evidence, the protection of the Fourth Amendment is of no value and might as well be stricken from the Constitution. The efforts of the courts are not to be aided by the sacrifice of those great principles established by years of endeavoring and suffering."

2. *Mapp v. Ohio* - 367 U.S. 643 (1961)

Quick Case Synopsis:

Cleveland Police Officers knock on the door of Dollree Mapp in search of a bombing suspect. Mapp is told by her lawyer not to let the police in without a warrant. The police eventually force their way past Mapp and enter the home. Mapp requests to see the warrant. The police flash a piece of paper that Mapp grabs and stuffs down her shirt. The police retrieve it and handcuff Mapp. They proceed to search everywhere for the suspect. During the search they find a chest that contained what amounted to pornographic materials - a crime in Ohio at the time. She is charged with the possession of obscene materials, convicted and sentenced even though the police never produced a copy of the "warrant."

Results of the Case:

- Mapp appeals to the State of Ohio
- The Ohio Supreme Court upheld her conviction which is later overturned by the U.S. Supreme Court
- The Supreme Court applied the Federal Exclusionary Rule to the States
- Any evidence obtained in violation of the 4th Amendment will be inadmissible in *any* (Local, State or Federal) court

Famous Quote from the case: Justice Thomas Clark

"We must close the only courtroom door remaining open to evidence secured by official lawlessness."

Fast Facts about Search Warrants

- The police must have PROBABLE CAUSE (PC) in order to obtain a search warrant (PC is also needed to make an arrest or to get an arrest warrant)
- The officer prepares a written affidavit
- The affidavit is sworn to before a judge and becomes a written order

- It must list the location to be searched and the persons or property to be seized—"The Elephant in the Ashtray"—the police can search anywhere that the object may fit. If I'm looking for a person, can I look in your sock drawer? No. But, can I look under the bed, closet or chest? Yes.
- The following are examples of the type of property that can be seized via a search warrant
  - o Stolen Property
  - o Property that was possessed unlawfully
  - o Contraband
  - o Property used or possessed for the purpose of committing or concealing a crime
  - o Evidence that points to an offense that was committed or that a person committed the offense
- In most jurisdictions search warrants must be executed within ten (10) days and between the hours of 0600 and 2100
  - o Unless a Nighttime Endorsement is provided
- The police must announce their presence by knocking on the door
  - o Unless a No-Knock Endorsement is provided
- The police can break in if necessary

To avoid confusion about search warrants and arrest warrants, because they are similar, here is a quick breakdown:

Arrest Warrant	Search Warrant
The officer must have probable cause	The officer must have probable cause
The officer prepares a written affidavit	The officer prepares a written affidavit
The officer swears in front of a judge	The officer swears in front of a judge
**Executable any time	**Executable between 0600 and 2100
**No expiration date	**Valid for ten (10) days

Exceptions to a Search Warrant

Every American has protection against "unreasonable searches and seizures," as per the 4th Amendment to the U.S. Constitution. The 4th Amendment states the following:

*"The right of the people to be secure in their persons, houses, papers, and effects, against unreasonable **searches** and **seizures**, shall not be violated, and no Warrants shall issue, but upon **probable cause**, supported by Oath or affirmation, and particularly describing the place to be searched, and the persons or things to be seized."*

A simple interpretation of the Amendment would be the following: A police officer develops probable cause that certain evidence exists at a certain location, swears to a judge who will determine if the officer in fact has probable cause, the judge signs off on the warrant and the officer will then execute the warrant. Unfortunately, the practical application of the 4th Amendment, as written, has little to do with any other types of interactions with the authorities outside of one's home. As you are aware, things such as cars did not exist at the time that Thomas Jefferson wrote the Constitution. So, case law decisions over the years have supplied law enforcement with the tools necessary to effectively do their jobs and balance the rights of citizens.

These court decisions, known as *stare decisis*, defined as the principal that the precedent decisions are to be followed by other courts, have lead to what law enforcement officers know as the exceptions to a search warrant. Searches without a warrant happen far more than those with a warrant as you will plainly see over the next few pages. These exceptions to a search warrant have also created strife between crime control advocates and civil libertarians. Crime Control Advocates view these decisions as a victory by allowing police to do their job and arrest criminals more effectively. Civil libertarians view them as eroding the foundation of an individual's civil rights and freedom.

The court decisions can be easily remembered with the help of the following acronym:

CHIP'S PEAS

    Consent
    Hot Pursuit
    Inventory
    Personal Garbage
    Search Incidental to Lawful Arrest

    Plain View
    Emergency Exception
    Automobile Exception
    Stop, Question and (Possibly) Frisk

- **Consent**

A person can waive their rights and give permission to an officer who does not have a warrant or probable cause, the authority to search their premise, person or vehicle. The person must have custody and control over the property. For example, your visiting friend cannot give the police permission to search your home, nor could your 9-year-old son. There are three (3) elements that must be present in order to have a legitimate waiver: the person must give up their rights: **VIK**

    Voluntarily
    Intelligently and
    Knowingly

In order to effectively control false allegations, investigators will provide a pre-printed department consent to search form that requires the individual to sign it. Remember, that the police cannot use trickery, intimidation or make threats to obtain the waiver. If they do, all of the evidence acquired will be thrown out.

- **Hot Pursuit**

The police can chase an individual wanted for a crime, anywhere they go (even someone else's home) as long as they maintain continuous sight. If the police lose sight of the subject and later develop information on where the person is, they must obtain a search warrant for that location. For instance, the perpetrator runs into a building with the police close behind. The perpetrator runs up a few flights of stairs and the police officer falls behind. The officer then hears a door slam, but doesn't know which apartment it was. The officer cannot start knocking down everyone's door. Even if a neighbor points to the door that the suspect ran into, the police would have to obtain a search warrant for that location or convince them to give up voluntarily.

- **Inventory**

In order to protect against allegations of wrongdoing, theft or damage, police departments have *established verifiable* procedures on what to do with property that comes into their custody (*South Dakota v. Opperman* 428 U.S. 364 1976). This procedure covers automobiles as well as other types of property that comes into the possession of the police department. Any contraband that is recovered during an inventory will be accounted for and criminal charges will be added to the docket. Even closed containers, such as a knapsack, briefcase, luggage, etc., can be opened and inventoried. The police cannot use this procedure to circumvent the establishment of probable cause. It is solely an administrative procedure.

- **Personal Garbage**

In the case *California v. Greenwood* 486 U.S. 35 (1988), it was decided that once a person abandons property by putting it in a location that everyone has access to (the curb), they forfeit their expectation to privacy. However, the police cannot come onto your property and search your garbage. Even though a homeowner must maintain the sidewalk and curb, they do not own it.

- **Search Incidental to Lawful Arrest**

Once a person is arrested lawfully the police can search their exterior and inside of their clothes. This is done for three main reasons: (1) officer safety, (2) prevent the destruction of evidence and 3) prevent escape. The police can also search the "lungeable" or "grabbable" area surrounding the person as well as any containers on or near the person (*Chimel v. California* 395 U.S. 752 1969).

- **Plain View**

An item which is observed by the officer and can be interpreted as being unlawfully possessed, can be seized without obtaining a search warrant, *as long as the officer has a lawful right to be at the location* (*Coolidge v. New Hampshire* 403 U.S. 443). For example, the police are called to a home where a domestic violence dispute took place. As the police are conducting the preliminary investigation, the officer sees a firearm on top of a nightstand. If it is an unlicensed firearm, the homeowner will be charged accordingly.

The Plain View Doctrine also applies to "open fields." An open field is any open, undeveloped land that is not used for a dwelling or a business. Even posted trespassing signs or fencing cannot stop the police from entering "open fields" if a crime is suspected.

- **Emergency Exception**

The police can enter a location where an emergency is or maybe occurring. The belief is that if the officer does not enter immediately a life can be lost, evidence can be destroyed or a suspect can escape (*People v. Mitchell* 39 NY 2d 173 (1976). The officer can search for additional victims or perpetrators and can seize anything in Plain View during the emergency, but cannot conduct a full search for evidence. In addition, officers are allowed to make a protective sweep of the location to ensure their safety by searching the house for additional people (*Maryland v. Buie* 494 U.S. 325 (1990). However, once the emergency is over, the officers will have to vacate the premise, secure it and obtain a warrant.

The courts also decided that there is no such thing as a "Murder Scene" exception. Three (3) decisions over the last thirty plus years, *Mincey v. Arizona* 437 U.S. 385 (1978), *Thompson v. Louisiana* 469 U.S. 17 (1984) and *Flippo v. West Virginia* 528 U.S. 11 (1999), have stated that once the emergency is over, or if a person of interest has an absolute right to privacy at the location, the police must obtain a search warrant. If not, any evidence obtained will be suppressed. Since most people are murdered by someone they know it is always a good decision to obtain a search warrant for the location, unless you know for sure that the victim lived alone.

- ## Automobile Exception

In *Carroll v. United States* 267 U.S. 132 (1925), the court decided that a warrantless search of a vehicle stopped in transit could be searched if the officer had probable cause to believe that the vehicle (including mobile homes) was transporting contraband or evidence. Because an auto is "mobile," evidence can be disposed of quickly while the officer attempts to get a warrant. An individual does not have the same right to privacy with their vehicles as they do their homes. In a recent Supreme Court decision in the case *Arizona v. Grant* 143 p.3d 379 (2006), the "police may search a vehicle without a warrant only when the suspect could reach for a weapon or try to destroy evidence, or when it is "reasonable to believe" there is evidence in the car supporting the crime (Newsday, April 22, 2009)."

Also, a police canine can sniff a vehicle as long as the officer had probable cause to stop the vehicle (*Illinois v. Caballes* 543 U.S. 455 (2005).

- ## Stop, Question and (Possibly) Frisk

Also known as the "Terry Stop" (*Terry v. Ohio* 392 U.S. 1 1968), was decided by the courts to protect an officer who may encounter a suspect with a weapon. The Terry Stop is a brief investigatory stop based upon REASONABLE SUSPICION that criminality is afoot. Note that I wrote possibly frisk. *It is not automatic.* An officer has to develop articulable facts that will allow them to pat down and reach into a suspect's clothing. Examples of an articulable fact can be the close proximity of a recent violent crime (murder, rape, robbery, felonious assault), clothing worn (heavy jacket in the summer) or a bulge.

State courts have made different rulings on what items can be searched for and/or removed. For instance, in New York, an officer can only reach into a suspect's clothing if they believe what they felt during a pat down was a weapon.

There are many case law decisions that changed the way the police deal with searches and seizures and the protections of the 4th Amendment. Crime Control advocates view these court decisions as dealing with the impractical and/or unsafe circumstances that police officers found themselves involved with every day.

Questions for Discussion and Review:

1. Why would the police want a Nighttime or No-Knock Endorsement?

2. The police obtain a search warrant for a home belonging to James Smith. The police have purchased drugs from the home on several occasions. When the police execute the warrant, they find more narcotics and arrest James Smith and his 80 year old mother Mary Smith. Why was Mary Smith arrested?

3. Can the police use ordinary citizens to obtain evidence for them? Why or why not?

4. What court case gave us the Federal Exclusionary Rule?

5. On January 10, 2007, the City of Jay obtained a search warrant for a known drug location based on probable cause. The City of Jay Police Department executed the warrant at 0700 hours on the morning of January 21, 2007 and recovered six (6) kilos of cocaine, three (3) handguns and one (1) semi-automatic machine gun. Should the Police Chief congratulate these officers for doing a fantastic job? In a sentence or two discuss your reasoning.

6. What court case applied the Federal Exclusionary Rule to the States?

7. Is an arrest a seizure and therefore covered under the 4th Amendment? Explain why or why not.

8. Are the police allowed to chase an individual across state lines that went through a red light?

9. If a police officer observes a bullet in the back seat of a car, can he/she search the entire car?

10. In order to give consent an individual must do it
_____, _____ & _____.

11. Do you feel that "exceptions" to a search warrant erodes the value of the U.S. Constitution?

12. The police respond to a house about a lost child. While they are inside of the house, one of the officers opens a cabinet and finds an unregistered pistol. The homeowner is arrested. Would the pistol be admissible in court? Why or why not?

13. In order for a Plain View seizure of evidence to be admitted in court, the police must be there how?

Chapter 4

The Crime Scene Protocol

"Oh, how simple it would all have been, had I been here before they come like a herd of buffalo and wallowed all over it."

— Sir Arthur Conan Doyle:
The Boscombe Valley Mystery

If criminal investigation was an automobile, the crime scene would be the engine that powered it. Without a good engine, the car goes nowhere. A crime scene is the location where a crime was committed. It can only occur in two (2) locations: Inside and Outside. Inside crime scenes are easier to maintain because you can keep most people out by shutting a door or blocking an entrance. The real reason cops love indoor crime scenes is that they offer lots of protection against the elements. Outdoor crime scenes are more difficult to secure because of their sheer size and lack of physical boundaries. Mother Nature can be very unfriendly to the investigator.

Weather is only one of the many uncontrollable occurrences known as evidence dynamics. The concept of evidence dynamics is defined as, "any influences that adds, changes, relocates, obscures, contaminates, or obliterates physical evidence, regardless of intent" (Chisum & Turvey, 2006). An investigator must make allowances for evidence dynamics that occur before, during and after a criminal event. For example, the first police officers on the scene may step on, kick or destroy physical evidence unintentionally. Investigators must keep this in mind, especially when conducting the initial interviews with responding officers.

Crime scenes are extremely important to the investigator because that is where you will find your physical evidence. The investigator must keep in mind that other crime scenes, a secondary or tertiary, may exist. The location where the crime occurred is the primary crime scene, unless you are investigating a homicide, then it is where you find the body. For example, a body is found out in the woods with multiple stab wounds, but very little blood. The "dump" site becomes your primary scene even though the act was committed somewhere else. An investigator can reach this conclusion based on the seriousness of the wounds. If an individual suffered multiple stab wounds, one would find a lot of blood at the scene. Sometimes, you will never find the location where the incident took place. The area where the crime was committed, or where the body was found, will be labeled the inner perimeter and the area that surrounds the crime scene will be the outer perimeter. Both have to be secured and cordoned off. No one but necessary personnel, the case investigator, the investigating supervisor and crime scene unit personnel will be allowed in the inner perimeter.

As you will see over the next couple of pages, a lack of crime scene control can have disastrous effect on the outcome of the case. The investigator must take their time and process the scene properly—you get only one chance to do it right—there are no second chances!

My experience as a detective supervisor and instructor, has led me to create a crime scene protocol using the acronym, **CRIME SCENE**. Each letter stands for the basic steps the investigator needs to take (in order) during a major criminal event. Like them or not, police department lingo is littered with acronyms, and I believe, ones that are easy to remember, work. Every department has a person locked in the bottom of headquarters whose sole job is to discover new acronyms! I'm only kidding.

Collect all of the information you can before leaving the station house

Reassess the crime scene boundaries set up by the patrol officers upon arrival at the scene

Initiate the crime scene walk-through with the first officer on the scene as your guide

Make extensive notes at the crime scene

Everything must be photographed

Sketch and search the crime scene

Collect and record physical evidence discovered at the scene

Evidence chain of custody is paramount to ensure a professional investigation

No stone is to be left unturned

Exit strategy

Collect all of the information you can before leaving the station house.

Detective Smith is sitting at his computer typing a report when the phone rings. Sgt. Jones tells him that a woman was found dead in the park. What does Detective Smith do first? Det. Smith records the time of the notification and the identity of the person that notified him of the incident. Investigators can be notified of a crime scene in the following ways: (1) a direct notification from patrol officer/supervisor at the scene, (2) through the Desk Officer or (3) by police radio transmission. The notification to the investigator begins the investigative timeline. The investigator must prepare from this point on as if the case is going to court.

The investigator must find out if the victim is still at the scene. If not, what hospital where they transported to? An investigator should be dispatched immediately to the hospital in an attempt to interview the victim or to obtain a dying declaration. In order to obtain a valid dying declaration, the individual has to believe that they are about to die. The investigator at the hospital should obtain custody of the victim's clothes for future forensic analysis: body fluids, gun shot residue (GSR), physical evidence, personal property, cell phone, identification, etc.

An all out effort must be made to identify 911 callers and conduct basic computer checks on both the caller if known and any information they have received. For example, run the address to determine what types of calls for police service originated from the location in the past. Where there an unusual number of "gun runs" at the location or numerous calls regarding drug sales? Or is there a history of calls for domestic violence? Many cases have been solved before the detective ever left the stationhouse. Many times an investigator must obtain a subpoena for the phone company in order to obtain subscriber information.

911 callers play a pivotal role in the investigation because they are your eyewitnesses to the event in question. If someone made the effort to notify the police, they did so with trepidation. Therefore, interviewing them away from the scene is a good idea.

Armed with some background information about the case, the investigator must take some equipment with them to the scene. Business cards for leaving with witnesses or during canvasses, a digital camera, crime scene tape (you can never have enough of it), cell phone, a police radio, a flashlight and a new notepad.

Reassess the crime scene boundaries set up by the patrol officers upon arrival at the scene.

Patrol officers are the individuals that determine the overall size of the crime scene, not the investigator. Hopefully, they make the determination based on the information they received during the preliminary investigation. The rule is to make the crime scene as big as you can; it can always be made smaller. You have to ask yourself, "is the crime scene big enough?" If possible, you, the investigator, will expand the boundaries. Next, ask yourself, "Is this the primary crime scene?" It may not be, so identify secondary or tertiary scenes and make sure they are properly secured. Fire escapes, back alleys or any egress that the perpetrator could have used to escape should be secured as "extended" crime scenes. Is the crime scene properly delineated so onlookers are kept out? Is this incident likely to attract media attention? Do we need to establish an area for the media? Where do we want to put the media? Ideally, we want to put them close enough so that they feel they are part of the investigation, but far enough away that they don't get in the way. The investigator should ensure that crime scene tape and other barriers are up to prevent any unauthorized personnel from gaining access to the scene.

The investigator should look for a location, away from the inner perimeter of the crime scene, to establish a temporary headquarters if one hasn't been set up already. The temporary headquarters can be used to plan how things will be conducted and provide a level of shelter from the weather. Many departments now have mobile temporary headquarter vehicles equipped with phones, wireless laptops, printers, fax machines and most importantly, bathrooms.

In hours of darkness, request a support unit, i.e., SWAT, ESU, etc., that has moveable lighting to help with the search. If necessary the police can ask a local utility or construction company for moveable lighting. Flashlights alone will not be sufficient lighting for a crime scene investigation!

All crime scenes must have a patrol officer posted to act as the "gatekeeper." The role of the gatekeeper is to prevent access to the crime scene by unauthorized persons and non-essential personnel and to maintain a record of the identity of those who entered the scene. This record must be secured and placed in the case file for possible use in the courtroom. Generally, police officers will stay out of the crime scene when their names are being recorded so they do not receive a subpoena to testify in court.

Crime Scene Survival Tip

Always double your crime scene tape boundary with an upper and lower "railing." Do this for both the inner and outer perimeters. You ask why? So you can keep police personnel out of your crime scene. They can decide if they should go over it or under it. Unauthorized police personnel in a crime scene can contaminate it and destroy valuable physical evidence.

Once you are confident that the crime scene is secured, you must turn your attention to the many individuals that must be interviewed. In person interviews at the crime scene whenever possible should be conducted. Here is a list of individuals that must be interviewed:

- First officer(s) on the scene
  - What were their observations upon arrival at the scene?
- Did they observe anyone/vehicle fleeing the scene?
  - Where did they enter the scene?
  - Did they touch anything at the scene?
  - Did they detain anyone at the scene?
  - Did they let anyone leave the scene?
  - Did they use the bathroom? Smoke at the scene? Use the phone at the scene?
  - Was anyone overly helpful upon your arrival at the scene?
- Victim/Witnesses
  - Interviews must be conducted before the person's memory begins to fade or they get tainted by others
  - Separate victims/witnesses so they do not confer with one another

o   Properly identify each person interviewed
- Pedigree information: name, address, date of birth, phone number, employment information, etc.
- Use photo identification
- EMS personnel
  o   Did they touch anything at the scene?
  o   Did they move the body?
  - What was their reason for moving the body?
- Fire department personnel
  o   Is the fire suspicious? Why?
- Medical Examiner/Coroner/Medico Legal Investigator (MLI)
  o   What is their assessment of the situation?

At this time the investigating supervisor will make assignments. He/she will use a large flip chart or whiteboard to list the locations and the names of the investigators who will respond (see Figure 4.1). Tight controls must be kept on who is where and doing what. This practice will prevent cross contaminating scenes—a major problem in the O.J. Simpson case.

> **Crime Scene Management Tip**
>
> Use a flip chart to keep track of investigators and their assignments

Figure 4.1

Homicide #6 I/S/O 123 150th St Apt 2A		
Osorio/Hernandez	C/S	123 150th St 2A
Padilla/Tebbens	Veh.	C/O 150 & 149
Dalton/Mosner	Canvass	123 150th St
Honora/Bone	Standby	
Berger	Squad Room	

In the event that another crime scene is located, which two detectives will be excluded from it?

Initiate the crime scene walk-through with the first officer on the scene as your guide.

The investigator must make sure they follow the same path in and out of the scene that they originally used. If possible, think about cordoning off the pathway so all necessary police personnel can access the scene without destroying evidence. The purpose of a crime scene walk-through is to identify what physical evidence exists in the scene and to determine if there is a possibility that the evidence can be destroyed. For instance, you have an outdoor crime scene and it begins to snow heavily. The weather factor is your biggest threat to an outdoor crime scene. The investigator has to act quickly or risk losing the evidence forever. This is not the ideal situation when working with crime scenes.

After completion of the crime scene walk-through, the detective should begin to formulate their investigative hypotheses. An investigative hypothesis is an assumption, or educated guess, of what is believed to have occurred based on the crime scene, the physical evidence, witness/victim statements and the preliminary investigation conducted by the patrol officer. I am a firm believer that generally investigators piece together what had occurred and who did it in the first five minutes, but spend the rest of the time proving it. The investigator begins to build his/her hypothesis on how and why the crime was committed at this point. Sometimes the "why" is more important that the "how." The "why" is the motive behind the crime. Identify the motive and you can establish a list of suspects. Investigators rely on the fact that most people are killed by someone they know. The closest people to the victim are always suspected first. The investigator attempts to establish the elements of a suspect through the closet person in our lives: **MOM**

Means - was the person physically capable of carrying out the crime?

Opportunity -was the suspect available to commit the crime? Do they have a rock solid alibi?

Motive - Was it over what I refer to as the Homicide Triangle: Love, Money or Drugs? Why would somebody want this person dead?

The investigator needs to be careful not to marry the hypothesis. It is alright to be wrong, but be flexible. When the facts and circumstances lead you in another direction, do not fight it just to be right. Criminal investigations have no room for egos.

Make extensive notes at the crime scene.

Document the time you arrived at the scene for a continuation of the investigative timeline. What was the weather like? What were your observations? What information did you receive from your in-person interviews (see "Reassess the crime scene boundaries...")? This information may prove or disprove a suspect's alibi in the future. In many jurisdictions these notes must be kept in the case folder as per the "Rosario Material" ruling (*People v. Rosario* 9 NY2d. 286 1961). A new notebook should be used for each major investigation and preserved for a future criminal trial. Never tear any pages out of the notebook!

Crime Scene Survival Tip

Before using a new notebook, check how many pages are supposed to be in the book and then count them. If a page is missing, do not use the book!

Notes serve several purposes for the investigator. Notes for an investigator are indeed a good **CHAP**.

Create a written historical record of the event
Help write the initial investigative report
Act as a memory aid in courtroom testimony
Preserve information for statistical purposes

Everything must be photographed and detailed on a Photographic Log

Ideally, the scene should be photographed before any evidence is collected. In the real world this may not be such a reality. For instance, the likelihood of leaving a firearm on the street during an investigation may not be in your best interest. First, it can be used against you or another officer at the scene, or it can be easily stolen during the commotion and confusion that often takes places at a crime scene. If evidence is in danger of being stolen, have a patrol officer stand near the object until it can be properly documented. This tactic only works if the department has ample personnel.

It is always better practice to take more photos then less. Photos provide an accurate historical record of the scene. Photos of the scene are taken in three steps:

(1) Far away to give an overall view of the scene
(2) A medium range and
(3) A close up.

Crime Scene Survival Tip

Do not take crime scene photos with investigators standing around in the background. The presence of investigators in the photos can be seen as a lack of crime scene management.

At least two sets of photos will be taken of physical evidence before it is collected. The first photo will be of the object *in situ* (Latin for in place). The next photograph will have a scale or ruler placed near the object. The ruler gives us the accurate size and reference. The reason you take the photo without the ruler first is because you are altering the crime scene by introducing the ruler.

All photographs have to be accounted for on a Photographic Log or similar evidence collection form. The Photographic Log should have the following information:

- Name and department identification number of the photographer
- Address of the crime scene
- Case number
- Crime Scene Unit 's number
- Time and date
- Weather conditions
- Photograph number(s)
- Type of film and camera used

If possible, a videographer should be used to video tape the entire crime scene in addition to the taking of crime scene photos. Video can prove to be an invaluable piece of demonstrative evidence in the courtroom and also provide investigators an opportunity to "re-visit" the crime scene at a later date. This can be extremely important when investigators are transferred, retired or when the case goes cold. Today's ever changing technology makes this an easy option to use and store video evidence.

Sketch and search the crime scene.

There are two (2) categories of crime scene sketches:

    (1) the Rough Sketch and
    (2) the Smooth Sketch.

You do not have to be Pablo Picasso to draw the rough sketch of a crime scene, but is extremely important. The Rough Sketch can be drawn in your notepad so that it is preserved forever. The sketch must have the day, date, time, location, case number and the investigator's name.

The smooth sketch can be drawn either by hand or be computer generated. This is the sketch that will be used to demonstrate in court. So an artist or cartographer should be used from within the department. Make sure it is an accurate account and do not make any changes to it once you leave the scene. All sketches must have a legend explaining the sketch as well as a North compass point. Write the investigative report regarding the sketch and account for it as an attachment for that report, and file it in the case folder.

Crime scene sketches serve many purposes. But if you want **PEACE** and quiet in your squad room, then make sure one is done. The following are benefits an investigator possess from using a sketch:

Permanent record of the scene
Eliminates the clutter often associated with lots of photographs
Admissible in court as demonstrative evidence
Creates a mental picture for those who were not at the crime scene (jurors)
Establishes the precise location and relationship of object and evidence

Once the location has been photographed and sketched, now the investigator or crime scene technician will employ the appropriate crime scene search method for the scene. There are five (5) ways to search a crime scene, but in my opinion, two of them, the Spiral Search (Figure 4.2) and Pie/Wheel Search (Figure 4.3) are not practical or effective. The only thing missing in the Spiral Search is a blindfold and a pin the tail on the donkey. The Spiral Search is supposed to be used in the event where only one searcher is available. If a supervisor insists that a Spiral Search be used, the investigator will start at the outer rim and make their way to the core of the crime scene. The Pie/Wheel Search is not practical because it breaks the crime scene up into "slices of pizza," which makes it difficult to cordon off the area.

An investigator is better off using either the Strip/Line Search (Figure 4.4) or the Grid Search (Figure 4.5). The Strip/Line search is conducted with a number of searchers "shoulder to shoulder" walking down a straight path. The Grid Search is more time consuming because the investigator redoubles the effort. But, they also double the chance of discovering evidence. A Zone Search (Figure 4.6) would be more practical in large open areas, such as an open field or large park. A zone is created and broken up into smaller more manageable scenes, usually four quadrants. Within each of the zones, either the Strip/Line or Grid Search would be employed.

If a searcher encounters evidence during any of the above search methods, all searching will stop momentarily until a decision is made on how the evidence will be handled. The time of day, weather factors and the risk of loss, will play the dominant role in the decision making process.

Figure 4.2 - Spiral   **Figure 4.3 - Pie Wheel**

Figure 4.4 - Strip/Line Search   Figure 4.5 - Grid Search

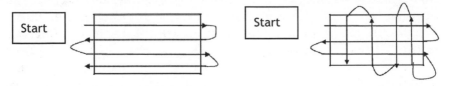

The Strip/Line Search (Figure 4.4) has officers or searchers standing shoulder to shoulder down a lane - like a race track. The Grid Search (Figure 4.5) is the most time consuming of all the methods, but you also have the best chance of recovering evidence.

Figure 4.6 - Zone Search

A	B
C	D

Remember, one of the search methods will be used inside each of the "zones"

Collect and record physical evidence discovered at the scene.

What is physical evidence? Physical evidence is anything that can prove that a crime was committed. It is also known as real evidence. Physical evidence is evidence that can be seen and held and can come in different forms such as solids, liquids etc. Physical evidence can come from **CVS**: the

Crime scene
Victim
Suspect

What is the value of physical evidence? Physical evidence comes in two (2) distinct categories of characteristics:

(1) Class Characteristics and
(2) Individual Characteristics.

The investigator has to realize that all objects have both class and individual characteristics. It will be the task of the investigator or forensic scientist to distinguish the two. Class characteristics are qualities that are shared by a group of objects. For instance, a group of 38 caliber firearms have class characteristics. They all hold the same size cartridge and they are all used to shoot the same size bullet. But is every 38 caliber the same? No. Individual characteristics are exactly as the word "individual" implies: that each piece of evidence has a unique characteristic, no two are alike. Fingerprints, DNA and the 38 caliber's barrel from the example above, will make unique striation marks on a fired bullet. Therefore they have Individual Characteristics.

What can physical evidence do? An investigator who knows the importance of physical evidence in a crime scene **DRILLS** down to the truth! Physical evidence can do all of the following:

Determine whether a crime was committed
Reconstruct the crime scene
Investigative leads provided
Link a suspect to a victim and/or crime scene
Link serial crimes
Suspect & witness statement corroboration

Identifying physical evidence from the above sources falls under the theory of transfer known as Locard's Exchange Principle. In 1920, Edmond Locard suggested that when two objects come together, something is exchanged between and taken away by both objects (Turvey, 2008, p. 8-9).

The following quote taken from the seminal text on criminal investigation, entitled, Criminal Investigation by Paul Leland Kirk (p. 4). It sums up the importance of Locard's Exchange Principle and the importance of physical evidence:

"Wherever he steps, whatever he touches, whatever he leaves - even unconsciously - will serve as silent evidence against him. Not only his fingerprints and his shoe prints, but also his hair, the fibers from his clothes, the glass he breaks, the tool mark he leaves, the paint he scratches, the blood or semen he deposits or collects - all of these and more bear mute witness against him. This is evidence that does not forget. It is not confused by the excitement of the moment. It is not absent

because human witnesses are. It is factual evidence. Physical evidence cannot be wrong; it cannot perjure itself; it cannot be wholly absent. Only in its interpretation can there be error. Only human failure to find, study, and understand it can diminish its value."

Locard's Exchange Principle is especially true in cases where a violent struggle took place. The chances of obtaining transfer samples in this type of event from the suspect are much greater. This is why proper controls at crime scenes are important so contamination can be avoided. For example, an investigator is inside of a crime scene conducting an investigation. During the investigation, the police develop probable cause to arrest the boyfriend. The investigator arrives at the boyfriend's house and arrests him. Do we see a problem? You should, because the investigator more than likely contaminated the boyfriend's house with evidence from the crime scene! A mistake like this could prove fatal in an investigation. This is why having a flip chart with everyone's assignments on it can be very useful.

Physical evidence that may contain physiological fluids (blood, semen, saliva, etc.) should be given the opportunity to air dry if possible before they are packaged. Any evidence containing physiological fluids (therefore possible DNA) must be packaged in paper and NOT plastic and be stored in a cool dry place! If the evidence is not packaged properly, you run the risk of destroying it. Most other types of evidence can be packaged in a suitable container or security-type envelope. DNA evidence must never be left in direct sunlight or inside of a hot vehicle.

Remember, the investigator is in charge of the scene. If you want something dusted because you believe it may reveal prints, ask the technician. It is not a good time to be shy; you may overlook a valuable piece of evidence. If you have a hunch, go with it. If the evidence is never recognized, recorded and packaged, it will be lost forever!

There is a proper order to process the crime scene. Here is a quick reminder not to forget to hit the **ESC** key:

Everything must be photographed
Sketch the crime scene - then search
Collect the evidence for packaging

CI Tip Sheet

Photograph ➤ Sketch ➤ Search ➤ Collect

Evidence chain of custody is paramount to ensure a thorough and professional investigation.

The chain represents the written, chronological and unbroken history of who found the evidence and where it was found. It is all about accountability and therefore will be the first part of the investigation attacked by the defense attorney. The chain of custody also records any changes in the evidence. For example, the lab may need to use some of the drugs recovered to conduct tests. Many cases have been lost do to poor or no chain of custody. You do not want to be the one on the witness stand trying to explain why evidence is unaccounted for. Remember, each person that comes into contact with the evidence creates a new "link in the chain." Links should be kept to the minimum. An evidence chain of custody could look like this: The Crime Scene Investigator ➤ An Evidence Property Control Officer ➤ the Police Laboratory ➤ The Medical Examiner's Office/DNA Laboratory (if necessary).

No stone is to be left unturned.

Anything and everything can be evidence. If it caught your attention, it may be significant. When in doubt, "bag it and tag it," and never overlook the obvious. In addition, make sure that the body is thoroughly searched for identification. I have been an observer at the medical examiner's office when an unidentified body is delivered, only for the ME to reach into the back pocket and remove the victim's wallet. The investigator was very embarrassed. Do not let it be you!

Exit strategy.

Plan to release the crime scene only after a thorough search has been conducted and all debris left by emergency personnel is disposed of and removed. If possible have EMS police up their personal protective equipment (PPE). The case investigator should confer with the investigating supervisor before the final determination is made to release the scene.

If the crime occurred at night and there is a reasonable chance of good weather, it is best to wait until the morning to search the scene before releasing it. Daylight is better than any flashlight or floodlight.

Now that you have been introduced to the investigative techniques in **CRIME SCENE** that are used to secure crime scenes, preserve evidence and solve crimes, here is one more acronym to hammer the rules home. If an investigator has to, he/she must **CAMP** out at the crime scene to make sure that it is done properly.

Conceptualize the scene
Apply inclusiveness
Maintain documentation
Proceed cautiously

Conceptualize the scene

The investigator builds hypotheses on how the crime was committed, but, always keeps in mind the possibility of being wrong. When the evidence and information develop, your hypothesis may/may not have to be adjusted. It's OK to be wrong. The only fault you can make is not admitting it and continuing to push the facts to match the theory. The investigator should think of questions such as these: "What is here?" "What is missing?" "What am I missing?" "What is out of place?"

Apply inclusiveness

Anything and everything can be important to the investigation. If you think it is evidence, treat it as if it was by collecting and packing it properly. No one is going to fault you if you took something that did not amount to anything, only if you didn't. You can't shout, "Do over!" Remember, not everything is what it seems to be.

Inclusiveness has to do with other matters as well. Don't be lazy. If another investigator or even family of the victim stated they did something, double check. Think of the Jon Benet Ramsey case where the father told the police he had searched the house, only to find the body hours later. The investigator should spare himself/herself and the department the embarrassment. Also, it is extremely important to obtain elimination prints/swabs from members of the same household so you don't waste your time running prints through AFIS or DNA through CODIS. It is a waste of money, effort and most importantly, a waste of valuable time.

Maintain documentation

Case documentation is like the old saying about purchasing a house, "Location, location, location." The same theory applies to criminal investigation: "Document, document, document." Even if you applied inclusiveness and identified, collected and packaged the evidence correctly, without proper documentation, you will lose the chain of custody, lose the evidence and therefore lose the case. The investigator is responsible for either completing or collecting **CAPE**:

Crime Scene Entry/Exit Log
Assignment Sheets
Photographic Log
Evidence Collection Log

Proceed cautiously

Haste makes waste. Whoever said that must have been referring to crime scene investigation. Crime scenes take time if done properly. Weather conditions can cause angst for investigators, but items such as tents can mitigate damage from such an event. As a reminder when conducting the crime scene walkthrough, ask the first officer on the scene to show you how they entered, so that you do not destroy anything else.

It is human nature to be drawn straight to the body of a homicide victim. You have to fight that instinct because generally the area surrounding the body will have the most forensic evidence. If an investigator has tunnel vision, he/she may miss or destroy valuable evidence.

Here is a quick breakdown on the duties of a patrol officer (first responder) and the duties of an investigator at a crime scene. In many police departments across the country, lack of personnel may be an issue. In some cases, the first responder may also be the case investigator and the crime scene technician!

The Patrol Officer	The Investigator
Records time of notification & arrival	Records time of notification & arrival
Establishes the size of the crime scene	Expands the crime scene (if possible)
Enters scene through a single entryway	Conducts crime scene walkthrough
Primary function is to protect life	Primary function is to ID evidence
Establishes temporary headquarters	Establishes temporary headquarters if not done
Conducts the Preliminary Investigation	Conducts the Follow Up Investigation
Detains witnesses/victims	In depth interviews with witnesses/victims
Secures the crime scene	In charge of the crime scene
Acts as the gatekeeper	Conducts the crime scene walkthrough
Maintains the crime scene log	Retrieves the crime scene log

Questions for Discussion and Review:

1. Has physical evidence replaced the need for eyewitness testimony? Explain why or why not.

2. Photographs from a crime scene are recorded on the _____.

3. Why is it so important for investigators not to contaminate a crime scene?

4. What is the correct order for processing a crime scene?

5. Who is in charge of the crime scene?

6. In order to properly document a crime scene, what are the four (4) logs that must be used?

7. Explain the purpose of the gatekeeper.

8. Why is a ruler used in crime scene photographs?

9. Explain the importance of an investigative timeline.

10. What are evidence dynamics and what role can they play in the criminal investigation process?

11. Name other occurrences that can be evidence dynamics other than the examples provided in the text.

12. Who makes the decision to release the crime scene?

13. Why are crime scene sketches important to investigations?

14. Make a list of physical evidence that an investigator can find at the crime scene and explain what individual & class characteristics they have.

15. Why don't the police use chalk to outline bodies like they do on television?

16. Where are the only two (2) locations where a crime scene can be?

17. What are the three elements that must be established in order to have a viable suspect?

Chapter 5

The Follow Up Investigation

"Everyone is somewhere."
— Joseph Reznick

Depending on the incident, the follow up investigation begins either directly at the scene or a few days later after the case has passed a solvability test. The follow up investigation begins where the patrol officer's preliminary investigation left off. Sometimes, the leads are few and far between and sometimes the leads go dead real fast. An investigator has to develop new leads quickly. The follow up investigation requires a lot of digging, sifting and disseminating of information. Think of the investigator as an archaeologist who digs up the past, finds artifacts and puts together pieces of an ancient civilization.

Therefore, the investigator must perform immediate **CPR** on the case:

Canvasses
Police record checks
Reexamination of physical evidence

Canvasses

Investigators will begin canvassing the neighborhood shortly after their arrival to the scene and have been given a chance to confer with the first officer(s) on the scene. It is important to have the preliminary facts surrounding the case so the investigators know what questions to ask or what types of canvasses to conduct. When an investigator is prepared and knows the preliminary facts of the case they can identify any deception or an outright lie. Investigators can then zone in on a particular individual and why they lied. Are they protecting themselves or someone they know?

Canvasses should always begin at the crime scene and spiral outward. In Figure 5.1 the apartments facing the courtyard would be canvassed first. The nice thing about conducting canvasses is that the same rules apply to both apartment buildings and private homes. So it doesn't matter if the crime happened in a rural or urban area, they are both conducted the same way.

Figure 5.1

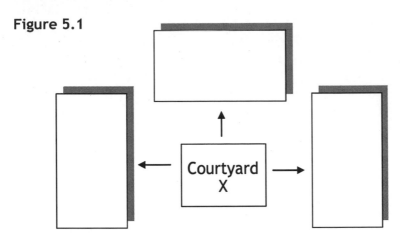

During the canvass, investigators will speak to anyone and everyone who will listen. They will speak to letter carriers, construction workers, dog walkers, homeless people, prostitutes, confidential informants, parolees, delivery workers and even at times drug dealers. No one can be left out. Where do you start in a building? There are no rules for starting at the bottom and working your way up or vice versa. You can just pull up in from of the building and wait for the first curtain to move. That is the LOL. LOL is not what you guys know it as. The nosey little-old-lady (LOL) who just moved the curtain may have also witnessed the incident. Every building and every neighborhood has one, so start there.

If an LOL does not live in the building, you can try the next best individual to speak with, the superintendent. The super of the building is attuned to the comings and goings of people in the building and can usually provide you with an apartment or family history. The super may also be able to provide you with a layout of the apartment, which can prove to be extremely helpful in developing a tactical plan to execute a search or arrest warrant.

Conducting a canvass is not always about knocking on doors and requesting information from people. There are other types of canvasses that exist and are sometimes overlooked during the commotion of a major criminal investigation. These canvasses, when conducted properly, can be extremely important to your case.

CI Tip Sheet

An artist paints on a canvas,
an investigator conducts a canvass.

Proper canvassing techniques will help investigators **SHAVE** hours off the investigative process (Giacalone, 2009, p. 8-9).

Surveillance Camera Canvass
Hospital Canvass
Additional witnesses
Vehicle Canvass
Evidence Canvass

Surveillance Camera Canvass

The use of surveillance cameras by both commercial and privately owned properties offers an investigator an invaluable source of information. The next best thing to being there when the incident happened is to get it on tape. In addition, to identify perpetrators, video evidence can also identify witnesses, key physical evidence and may assist in processing the crime scene, as well as assist in the interrogation of suspects.

The investigator should be aware of the following potential problems: proprietary software - the tape may not work on your equipment, a lack of knowledge by the end user (i.e., store clerk), the tape/video is recorded at another site, and the famous, no video/DVD in the machine. Competition has made the technology much cheaper now and investigators are finding video surveillance evidence in residential properties as well.

> ### CI Case Study
>
> All video has "value." No matter how dark, fuzzy or blurry the video is, the perpetrator can still be identified. It may be by a piece of clothing, hat, jacket or piece of jewelry or in one case I had, one of the perpetrators in a vicious murder was identified by a security officer by his discernable limp!

Hospital Canvass

It is quite possible that your suspect, or witness who does not want to be identified, has sought some sort of medical attention after an incident: a brawl, shooting, stabbing, gang fight, hit and run, etc. Often these individual(s) will drive to a hospital in another jurisdiction to throw off any suspicion. Therefore it is a go idea to expand your search beyond the immediate area.

Hospitals are required to notify the police whenever an individual enters the emergency room seeking assistance for a bullet wound, knife wound or any wound that is suspicious, i.e., chemical burns, explosives, etc. Each investigative squad should have a pre-printed Hospital Canvass form which can be faxed to all of the local area hospitals. The form should have the preliminary facts of the case, the types of injuries that may have been sustained and the investigator's contact information.

> ### CI Case Study
>
> After a multiple shooting at a night club, one of the perpetrators was shot in the foot and driven to the hospital by one of his friends. The friend drove up to the emergency room, dropped him off and then fled the scene. A careful examination of the surveillance tape revealed the license plate of the vehicle which led to an additional arrest.

Additional Witnesses Canvass

Locating additional witnesses are the main reason to conduct a canvass. An investigator should start at the scene of the incident and spiral outwards. This affords them a chance at inclusiveness. The skilled investigator interacts with and builds rapport to extract information from people who may otherwise be unwilling to provide it. At the very least, a canvass puts the community on notice that the police are seeking help in order to solve the crime. The canvass may generate an anonymous call into the squad or to the crime stoppers unit. In addition, a follow up canvass is extremely important and should be conducted 24 hours, seven (7) days, twenty-one (21) days and one (1) month after the incident. This way you can include individuals that may not visit or make deliveries everyday.

CI Tip Sheet

Canvasses are to be conducted:

1. As soon as practical upon arrival at the scene
2. 24 hours later
3. 7 days later
4. 21 days later
5. 1 month later

Vehicle Canvass

The vehicle canvass is a simple task that requires noting the license plates of vehicles in and around the area of a crime scene. A thorough review of a properly conducted vehicle canvass can prove or disprove a suspect's alibi or it can be used to find out where your target is laying his/her head. In addition, law enforcement officials have a tool called a License Plate Reader (LPR). The LPR records all of the license plates in the target area and provides a printout of the registered owners. They also provide GPS coordinates. In addition, license plate readers have been mounted on stationary poles on main roads and highways. LPRs can help an investigator identify witnesses and/or place a subject at the scene of a crime - or at least their vehicle. This information is discoverable for defense purposes and can provide additional witnesses or suspects.

CI Case Study

Are you working on a case that did not have a vehicle canvass conducted? Then try this.
Some municipalities allow you to pay your parking ticket online by punching in your plate number. If you know your target's vehicle information, enter it into one of these sites. This search can provide an investigator with the time, date, infraction and most importantly, the location.

Evidence Canvass

An investigator should never take for granted that all evidence has been identified and properly collected by the police in a criminal investigation. If possible, respond to the original location and conduct a search of the area. Have a plan for how and what you are going to search. If you find something that maybe evidence in a criminal investigation, photograph it in place (in situ) and notify the proper authorities so it can be "bagged and tagged."

Canvasses, if done properly, can yield the information required to successfully close a case or resurrect an old one. Each type of canvass should receive a separate investigator's report and be indexed for easy reference. Remember, the best investigative efforts will be lost if the information is not properly documented and recorded.

Police Record Checks

When a violent crime occurs, investigators have a series of tasks that they must perform. Today's investigator has a tool that wasn't available to them less than twenty years ago, the personal computer. Computers have replaced the typewriters and filing boxes. The computer has allowed police departments to access an array of databases, both public and private. These databases allow investigators to develop leads and establish linkage between people, places and things.

As discussed in the Crime Scene Protocol lesson, the investigator will retrieve information from the computer before leaving the stationhouse. Computer checks for 911 callers, on victims, perpetrators and possible suspects are an important investigative tool that may provide a lead in the case before they even start investigating! Databases also play a significant role in the hunt for a known perpetrator. When an individual is in trouble, who do they turn to? Yes, mom first then a girlfriend or relative. Wouldn't it be nice to have this information before traipsing all over the city or countryside for them? Investigative work is a lot like playing chess. You have to think two to three moves ahead of your opponent.

Computer checks are designed to aid investigators with establishing links between three (3) broad categories: (1) People, (2) Places and (3) Things.

(1) People

First and most importantly are the people involved in the incident. Since we are victimized by people we know most often, it is in the investigator's best interest to properly identify all of the players involved in the incident. In order to have a violent crime, you need a victim and a perpetrator. Each half makes the whole. Know the victim, and maybe you will identify the perpetrator.

Sometimes the victim can not tell us what happened for obvious reasons, i.e., deceased. Even if they could speak with us, they may leave out some pertinent artifact that they don't want anyone to know about. For example, hiding a certain person they are dating from their parents, an alternate lifestyle, a mistress, illicit drug use, gambling problem, nightclubs visited, etc. I think you are developing the picture. This is why the police will seek out family, friends and co-workers of the victim, especially if the victim is dead. People aren't too worried about passing along information that was held as a "secret." There maybe even a little guilt. Remember the famous quote from Benjamin Franklin, "Three people can keep a secret as long as two of them are dead." As an investigator wouldn't you like to speak with the victim's best friend? Contemplate a moment and think what type of information you shared in confidence with your best friend. Is it information that could land you on the front page of the papers? If so, you better be real nice to them!

The investigator will begin to create a cursory investigative timeline (Figure 5.2) of the incident and begin to input facts discovered during the investigation. Some investigators will plot the timeline of events on a flip chart or spreadsheet for easy reference. The next step is complete a series of computer workups on the victim. To an investigator this is known as Victimology, or "why was this person chosen."

Figure 5.2

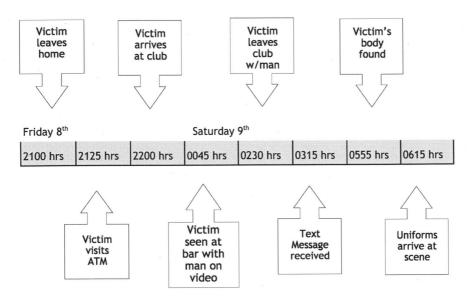

The investigator will attempt to complete at least a 24-48 hour time frame backwards from the incident in the hope of piecing together who the victim was with or where they went. The main focus of a victimology is to learn more about the victim then they knew or wanted to know about themselves. This two part process is accomplished through (1) computer inquiries and by (2) interviewing family, friends and co-workers. Is there anything in the victim's background that made them vulnerable?

Here are some questions you want answered about victims and witnesses through police computer inquiries:

- Did the victim have any previous contacts with the police?
    o Is their a current photo of the suspect available?
    o Previous arrest records can shed some light on the background of the victim
        - Were they ever arrested for assault?

- Were they ever arrested for dealing narcotics?
  - Who were their co-defendants?
  - Any gang affiliation?
  - Could the incident be narcotics related?
    - Can narcotics units provide some background on the subject(s)?
  - Were they in a fight?
  - Were they ever arrested for possessing a firearm?
- Did they ever file or have filed against them a Domestic Incident Report?
  - Did they have marital problems?
  - Were they in an abusive relationship?
    - Was there an order of protection? Valid? Expired?
  - Were any photos vouchered regarding domestic violence incidents?
- Does the victim have an active warrant?
- Was the victim wanted in connection with another crime?
- Have they been a victim of a crime recently?
  - Harassment/Stalking?
  - Robbery?
  - Burglary?
  - Sexual assault?
- Have they filed a report of lost property?
- Have they received any summonses?
  - Moving violations?
  - Criminal Court Violations?
    - What were the locations of these violations?
- Do they possess a valid pistol license?
- Was the victim ever an aided (person requiring medical attention - no crime) case?
  - What types of injuries, if any, were reported?
    - What hospital were they transported to?
- Was the victim the subject of a Stop, Question and Frisk Report?
  - What was the alleged crime?
  - What was the location?
  - Was anyone else stopped with them?
    - Conduct background checks on them

Here are some questions you want answered about perpetrators (if known) through police computer inquiries:

- Has the perpetrator ever been a victim before?
  - o What contact information did they provide back then?

CI Tip Sheet

When bad guys are victims they tend to provide accurate information including their correct name, date of birth (DOB) and address—including the elusive apartment number.

- Do they have any nicknames?
  - o Are records kept on nicknames?
- What previous arrest record does the perpetrator have?
  - o What type of crimes are they "in to"?
    - Street robberies or commercial robberies?
    - Burglary?
      - Burglars have been known to escalate to sexual predators
  - o Do they have a violent background?
  - o What contact information did they use on previous arrest records?
    - Phone numbers called?
    - Addresses and Apartment numbers used
    - Aliases
    - Social Security Number(s) used
    - Nicknames used
    - Tattoos, marks and scars
    - Gang affiliation
  - o Have they been arrested in other states?
    - Similar crimes?
      - Who were their associates?
      - Who bailed them out?
      - Who did they call from jail?
    - Check with NCIC and conduct an Offline Search

> ## CI Tip Sheet
>
> An NCIC Offline Search provides information on individuals that have been stopped by the police and either run in the system, summonsed or arrested. An Offline Search can track down an individual located in another state or to keep tabs on an individual while the investigator establishes probable cause to obtain an arrest warrant.

- o Have they received any criminal court summons for violations (non-crimes)?
  - What were the locations?
- o Was the perpetrator ever stopped, questioned and frisked?
  - Days, times, locations
    - Any location near the date and time in question?
- o Do they have any active warrants?
- o Are they wanted for other crimes?
  - Is any other law enforcement agency looking for him/her?
    - Make a coordinated effort and share information
- o Do they have any gang affiliation?
  - Which gang?
    - Is there any gang intelligence information?
- o Did they ever have a Domestic Incident Report filed against them?

> ## CI Tip Sheet
>
> Investigators count on relationship changes. Remember the old adage, "Hell hath no fury like a woman scorned?"

"Other" People

The following people can also be found in police computer database searches:

- 911 callers are your witnesses. In any given incident a number of people witness it, but few, if any report it.

That is why it is extremely important to locate, positively identify them interview them in person and take a statement. Has anyone ever called 911 who was actually the perpetrator? Yes, they have. Investigators must positively identify people with whom they are speaking. It is a terrible feeling to find out that the person you interviewed was the actual perpetrator and you failed to ID them!

- Parolees are an excellent source of information for one main reason, they must speak with police. If they refuse to cooperate, their parole can be violated, which means they will be sent back to prison
  o Parolees can also be a subject of the investigation themselves based on their previous crimes
    - For example, the police department may have a spike in sexually related crimes in the area - has anyone with that type of background been released back into society?
      - Certain levels of sex offenders must register with their local police precinct
- Active bench warrants from the area can be a source of information regarding the incident under investigation or the whereabouts of a known perpetrator. A bench warrant is issued when an individual fails to show up for their court date. Sometimes investigators have to "shake a few trees" to get the fruit to drop. Re-arresting persons wanted on bench warrants are "low hanging fruit," which means they are easily attained. But make no mistake about it, individuals wanted on active bench warrants can provide critical information.
- Confidential Informants (CIs) can act as the investigator's HUMINT (human intelligence) tree by providing information in real time. Generally, they help the police without anyone knowing. Their life depends on it.
  o The first thing any investigator must find out is why this person is willing to help me out? The two (2) main reasons people become informants are for (1) court consideration (time off or charges dropped) and (2) money. However, another motive exists that could be detrimental to your case, revenge. The investigator has

to know what an informant's motivation is before they are used.

o An informant and their information have to pass a two (2) prong test in many states, called the Aguilar–Spinelli Test (*Aguilar v. Texas* 378 US 108 (1964) and *Spinelli v. the United States* 393 US 410 (1969)). The first prong, is the informant reliable? and the second prong, is the information reliable? In *Illinois v. Gates* 462 US 213 (1983), the Supreme Court abandoned the two-prong test for a "totality of the circumstances test," which was adopted by several states. So depending on what state you work in, informants and their information are handled quite differently.

(2) Places

The location where the event occurred, either inside or outside, has to be examined as if it were a person. What type of location is it? Is it an apartment building or private house? Parking lot? Nightclub? etc. If we take a location such as a nightclub, what can that tell us? Information regarding the location can tell us what type of individual likes to frequent it and also it tells us about the lifestyle of the victim. In addition to lifestyle issues, it can also provide the motive behind the crime.

Here are some questions you want answered about commercial locations through police computer inquiries:

- Any previous calls for police service?
  - o Robberies?
  - o Fighting?
  - o Illegal narcotic sales/use?
    - Is it a known drug location?
    - Is there currently an active narcotics investigation?
      - Did they have any under covers inside of the location at the time of the incident?
  - o Prostitution?
  - o Underage drinking?
  - o Street parking conditions?
  - o Loud music?

CI Tip Sheet

Many nightclubs and bars have installed driver's license scanners at their establishments to prevent underage drinking. These scanners can provide a list of everyone that entered the location as well as provide a photo.

- Who is the owner?
  - o Do they have any arrest background?
    - Are they affiliated with anyone?
- Has the location been the subject of enforcement?
  - o Does the location have a liquor license?
- What is the capacity limit?

Here are some questions you want answered about *residential* locations through police computer inquiries:

- Who owns the property?
- Who lives at the location/house/apartment(s)?
  - o Are there any active warrants or wanted people attached to the address?
  - o Any parolees currently living at the location?
  - o DMV inquiries can provide a list of registered car owners
- Are there any past calls for police service?
  - o Any similar crimes occurred in the past?
    - Robberies?
    - Burglaries?
      - Does the homeowner have a residential burglary alarm permit?
    - Sexual assaults?
      - Check patterns
      - Any past search warrants executed at the location?
  - o Fighting?
  - o Drug sales?
    - Any open drug cases?
  - o Domestic violence?

(3) Things

The last category, Things, is a catch all for other objects that may be attributed to, used to escape with or linked to a specific person or place.

- Does the victim/perpetrator have any current/past vehicles registered to them?
  - What vehicles are registered to the home/apartment's address?
    - Any vehicle accidents in the past?
    - Do the vehicles have any summons activity?
      - Caught in red light camera traps?
        - What are the locations that summonses were issued?
- Are there any lawfully possessed pistols/long arms registered to the location?
  - Any reported lost/stolen?
  - Domestic violence history?
- Are there any phone numbers attached to anyone involved?
  - Were phone numbers ever used on police department records?
  - What locations do they come back to?
    - Subpoena records if necessary
      - Incoming and outgoing calls
        - Text messages
        - Photographs
        - Videos
- Electronic Toll records
  - Do Electronic Toll records support or discredit an alibi?
  - Do toll records establish the opportunity to commit the crime?
    - Subpoena records if necessary
- Train/Bus/Cab/Airplane Manifests
  - An alert can be put on the individual with the appropriate law enforcement agency, i.e., Port Authority, U.S. Customs, etc.

CI Tip Sheet

Electronic Toll programs have installed readers along many major highways that track vehicles from point to point. If the perpetrator's vehicle has an electronic toll device, there is a good chance investigators can subpoena the information.

Reexamination of Physical Evidence

When the case hits a snag, or there wasn't much information to go on to begin with, the investigator will sit down and take a fresh look at the following items: Crime scene photos/ video, the evidence log and the requests for lab testing (evidence submitted).

The investigator should find a nice quiet location and sort out the crime scene photos. The photo series should have begun with the front door (if inside) and walk you through the house, eventually landing where the body was located. The investigator thinks to themselves, "Did we miss anything?" If they are fortunate enough to have a video of the crime scene, they'll ask another investigator to watch it, who wasn't at the location in order to obtain an unbiased observation.

As the investigator views the photos/video, they will make a list of physical evidence as well as examine the scene for behavioral evidence. Sometimes a fresh look or a different theory on how/why the crime was committed is all that is needed. Do victim/witness accounts of the incident match up to what is observed in the crime scene? Perhaps some re-interviewing may be necessary.

Other than the case officer in a major case, investigators from other precincts and sometimes even different jurisdictions write reports for the case. The case investigator must ensure that those reports are accounted for, indexed and read. Was a lead developed by someone else and then lost in the confusion? A conferral must be made with those investigators to avoid missing critical information as well as avoiding duplicating efforts.

The evidence log is a chronological list of physical evidence that was recovered at the crime scene. It lists what type of evidence it is, who found it, who packaged it, who vouchered it and where did it go (police laboratory, medical examiner's office, etc)? Can the evidence in the crime scene photos/video or sketch be accounted for on the evidence log?

Not all evidence is going to require special examination and testing. After perusing the evidence log, the investigator must answer the following three (3) questions about the physical evidence recovered from the crime scene: (1) What type of evidence is it? (2) Where is it? and (3) What stage of analysis is it in?

There are several categories of physical evidence that require special laboratory testing. However, three (3) categories appear quite often: Fingerprints, DNA, and Ballistics. Fingerprints are loaded into AFIS, DNA into CODIS and Ballistics into IBIS (AFIS and CODIS were covered in Chapter 2). IBIS stands for the Integrated Ballistics Identification System which is coordinated by the Bureau of Alcohol Tobacco and Firearms (ATF). The goal of the IBIS database is to establish linkage between fired bullets and shell cases recovered from crime scenes to firearms and to link firearms removed from individuals to fired bullets and shell casings.

CI Cheat Sheet

AFIS - Fingerprints
CODIS - DNA
IBIS - Ballistics

It is the responsibility of the investigator to track down where evidence is, i.e., police lab or ME's office, and find out what stage of analysis the evidence is in. For example, was the DNA submitted to the local or national CODIS database? Is there a delay? Why is there a delay? Backlogs are not an uncommon problem. Is there an urgent need to have the DNA tested immediately? Crime labs can stop testing other evidence to work on an "emergency" request. What constitutes an emergency? A perpetrator that is on a crime spree, serial cases, cases that the perpetrator may flee the country, etc.

Hunting for a Known Perpetrator Checklist

- ☐ Records as a Victim
- ☐ Arrest Records
- ☐ Co-Defendant Records
- ☐ Domestic Incident Reports
- ☐ Stop and Frisk Reports
- ☐ NCIC Offline Search

Questions for Discussion and Review:

1. What type of information can family members tell an investigator about the victim?

2. Why is it important to identify previous locations where a wanted perpetrator was arrested?

3. Why is it important to find out if the perpetrator we are looking for was once a victim?

4. What is the significance of identifying parking summons activity on a particular vehicle?

5. Should the use of confidential informants be banned? Why or why not?

6. This type of canvass is the "door to door" request for information.

7. Why can some states not follow a Supreme Court ruling like in *Illinois v. Gates* (use of informant's information) and use their own standard?

8. Why do the police count on changes in people's relationships?

9. What can past calls for police service tell an investigator?

10. Canvasses should start at the incident and spiral
_____.

11. What role can a license plate reader (LPR) play in a criminal investigation?

12. What goal do the databases AFIS, CODIS and IBIS have in common?

13. How is a Hospital Canvass conducted? Why are they conducted?

14.   Why identify individuals wanted for warrants in a residential building that have nothing to do with the crime currently being investigated?

15.   List and explain what occurs in the five types of canvasses discussed in this chapter.

Chapter 6

Eyewitness Identification Procedures

"You did it because I said you did it!"

— Mom

Section 1 of the 14th Amendment to the U.S. Constitution states the following:

"...nor shall any State deprive any person of life, liberty, or property, without due process of law; nor deny to any person within its jurisdiction the equal protection of the laws."

The Due Process Clause is what protects the citizens of the United States from unfair police identification procedures that are too suggestive. Investigators must be mindful of these issues when using eyewitness identification procedures.

After a crime is committed, the police attempt to bring the victim to the person stopped or to the station house to view photographs. The idea is to use the person's memory of the event quickly before it fades. Eyewitness identification has been under attack now for several years, citing all types of experiments that showed that eyewitness accounts are not reliable. That is why it is extremely important to identify physical evidence of the crime and to seek out additional eyewitnesses who can corroborate what was observed. Single eyewitness cases with little or no physical evidence are extremely difficult to prosecute.

Unfortunately, the police have to rely on eyewitness identification because most of the time the victim is the only person who saw the perpetrator commit the act. More often than not, the victim never even gets a chance to see the perpetrator. Victims often do not see the perpetrator for the following reasons: the victim was approached from the rear, tunnel vision, victim was not paying attention (talking on phone, listening to MP3 player, etc.), out of fear, poor eyesight and even the weather can be a factor. Therefore, an investigator will make every attempt to identify physical evidence (see Chapter 2) and obtain surveillance camera footage when available (see Canvassing at the beginning of this chapter) from the crime scene to corroborate or disprove eyewitness accounts.

An investigator will employ **SAL** to help them with the three (3) eyewitness identification procedures: **S**how ups, **A**rrays and **L**ineups. **SAL** is also the proper order in which eyewitness identification procedures should be conducted.

Show-ups

A show-up is a prompt, on the scene viewing of a suspect one-on-one by the victim/witness. A show-up is often confrontational because the police detain a suspect based on a physical description broadcasted by the police from the victim/witness. The legal question that always arises is, "Do I take the suspect to the victim or do I take the victim to the suspect?" There is no answer to this question because it depends upon the circumstances. My experience has led me to believe that taking the victim to the suspect is far less suggestive than vice versa. But what happens if your victim is badly wounded? Then you have no choice but to bring the suspect to the victim, even if it is in a hospital (*People v. Johnson* 81 NY 2d 828 (1993).

Some of you may ask, "What gives a police officer the right to stop someone?" My question to you is, "What level of suspicion do the police have in that case?" Here is a review of previous material. A person matching a description provides a police officer with reasonable suspicion. What can the police do at reasonable suspicion? They can stop, question and (possibly) frisk. Not only does the person in this case match a description, but they are in close proximity of a violent crime. Would a reasonable person conclude that criminality was afoot? The only constraint is that a show up must be conducted within a reasonable amount of time, generally a few minutes, from the time of the initial incident (*Stovall v. Denno* 388 U.S. 293 (1967)).

CI Tip Sheet

The proper use of a show up can do two (2) things:
    (1) it can identify a suspect quickly
    (2) it can exonerate an otherwise innocent person

**A show up would never be used when a victim knows the suspect or if the suspect is already under arrest. When the victim knows the perpetrator it is fine to show a single photo to the victim in order to confirm the identify.

Arrays (AKA: Photo Arrays, Photo Lineup, Six-Pack)

An array, or photo array, is a procedure where the police have an idea who the perpetrator is, or have a detailed description, or the suspect has a certain modus operandi (MO). A photo array can only be used when the suspect *is NOT in custody*. If the suspect is in custody, the police must use a Lineup. If the victim/witness identifies the suspect in the array, the police now have probable cause to go out and make the arrest. Upon his/her arrest, the individual will then be put in a live lineup even though he was chosen in the array. However, if the victim/witness fails to pick the suspect out of the lineup, he/she will be set free and the investigation will probably be over.

With the advent of technology, constructing photo arrays has never been easier. Computer programs now exist that allow the user to input a description and create electronic arrays for viewing by the victim/witness almost immediately. When creating arrays the investigator must try to make it as fair and impartial as possible.

The police can use photographs from the **MOD S**quad's **FAVS**:

Mug books
Online mug books
Driver's license photos
Sex offender databases

Family photos
Arrest photos
Video cameras
Sketch artist

Guidelines for preparing an Array:

- Photo arrays are not to be used for "fishing expeditions"

- Sealed photos cannot be used (*United States v. Crews* 445 U.S. 463 (1980))
- A minimum of 6 photos (more can be used) will be used: one (1) suspect and five (5) fillers
- Each of the five (5) fillers will be of the same gender, age, race, physical makeup (*Grant v. City of Long Beach* 315 F. 3d 1081 (2002))
- Nothing in the suspect's photo can make them stand out: i.e., he/she is the only one wearing eyeglasses, has a big scar, mustache, bald, different colored background, etc.

Guidelines for showing the Array:

- Hand the array to the person so nothing can be suggestive about the array
- The investigator must explain to the victim/witness that the photos are in random order and that the perpetrator may or may not be included
- When the victim/witness "picks" the suspect, the investigator will have them sign their name under the photo: Identification = Probable Cause
- In instances where multiple victims/witnesses exist, each one will be shown the array separately. Also the police must make every effort to ensure that the victim(s) or witness(es) do not speak to one another
  o Additional arrays should be created with the perpetrator in different locations
- Never assist the victim/witness to pick anyone
- Never tell a victim/witness that they chose the "right" or "wrong" person
- The photo array used will be vouchered as evidence and kept with the case folder

Lineups (AKA Investigatory Lineup, Live Lineup, Simultaneous Lineup)

Lineups are used when a suspect is under arrest. The lineup procedure is very similar to the photo array, except that the individual is in custody. There are additional forms of lineups and there maybe issues that the police must deal with in regards to suspect's lawyers. Both will be addressed later in this section.

The lineup will be conducted in a room that has a one way mirror, with a shade, so that the victim/witness can view it without fear of being seen. To avoid problems, the perpetrator and fillers should be kept somewhere away from the viewing room. For the very first viewing (in multiple victim/witness cases) the victim/witness should be brought into the viewing room first and the door should be closed. If not, you run the risk of blowing your lineup.

Guidelines for Conducting Lineups:

- The case investigator, investigating supervisor and the assistant district attorney (ADA) will be present
  - o A lineup will never be conducted without a conferral with the ADA
- A minimum of 6 individuals (more can be used) will be used: one (1) suspect and five (5) fillers
  - o Police officers can be used as fillers as long as they are not wearing a uniform or other article of clothing that would identify them as the police
  - o If juveniles are needed, the police must obtain permission from a parent or guardian before using them
- Each of the five (5) fillers will be of the same gender, age, race, physical makeup and have similar dress
  - o Investigators usually have a collection of white t-shirts, black ball caps, etc. to make everyone "look" the same
  - o Each filler will also be instructed not to do anything that may single out the suspect, such as:
    - Directing eyes toward them
    - Head nodding
    - Finger pointing
- Nothing can make the suspect stand out: i.e., he/she is the only one wearing eyeglasses, has a big scar, mustache, bald, etc.
- The suspect is allowed to choose his/her place in the lineup: 1 through 6
  - o Each person will be given a placard with their number on it

o   In multiple viewings, the suspect can choose a
    different position each time
- Before the lineup begins a series of photos will be
  taken of the lineup to disprove claims of unfairness
- In instances where multiple victims/witnesses exist,
  each one will be shown the lineup separately. Also
  the police must make every effort to ensure that the
  victim(s) or witness(es) do not speak to one another
- Never assist the victim/witness to choose anyone
- Never tell a victim/witness that they chose the "right"
  or "wrong" person
- The investigator fills out a lineup report which is
  signed by the investigator, supervisor and in some
  jurisdictions the ADA too
  o   The lineup form records the identity of all who
      where present - including the names and pedigree
      information of the fillers
  o   The lineup form is secured with the case folder
      along with the photos and names and pedigree
      information of the fillers

Once the investigator is ready to start, he/she will say to
the victim/witness, "You are about to view a lineup. The
suspect may or may not be in the lineup. If you recognize
anyone, tell us who you recognize and where your recognize
them from." After that is said, the investigator will knock on
the glass and another investigator will open the shade. The
police can also make each individual in the lineup say a
phrase that the perpetrator used, "Your money or your life,"
for the purpose of voice identification.

When the viewing is over, the investigator will knock on
the glass again so that the shade can be drawn. The lineup
report will be completed as well as an investigator's report
detailing the events that transpired during the lineup and if
the victim/witness identified the suspect or not. A negative
report will also be written. "On (date, day of the week) at
(time), the victim, known to this Department, was unable to
identify a suspect in the lineup conducted at (location)."

> **CI Cheat Sheet**
>
> Number of Fillers in both an Array/Lineup = 5
> Number of Suspects in an Array/Lineup = 1
> Total = 6

Lawyer/Legal Issues

When we deal with eyewitness identification procedures, we have to be concerned with three Amendments: the 5th, 6th and the 14th. Parts of the 5th Amendment and the 14th Amendment's deal with due process, which simply state that the procedure be fair. The 6th Amendment deals with right to counsel issues. A suspect DOES NOT have an absolute right to counsel at an investigatory lineup (*Kirby v. Illinois* 406 US 682 (1972)), only at a post-indictment line up (*United States v. Wade* 388 US 218 (1967)). However, if a lawyer calls the police and states he/she wants to be present at the investigatory lineup, the police can grant them the request if practical. The lawyer will only be granted a reasonable amount of time, generally an hour, to arrive at the lineup location. If present, the lawyer can make suggestions regarding the lineup, but the police do not have to make any changes. Remember, the ADA will also be in the room, so the investigator will let the lawyers argue over it.

In a post-indictment lineup, the suspect is already represented by counsel, so they must be present at the lineup. A post indictment lineup is usually scheduled on a pre-arranged date and time between the ADA and the suspect's lawyer. One caveat about a post-indictment lineup, the police CANNOT question the suspect on anything, he has a lawyer!

Other Types of Lineups

Other types of lineup identification exists other then the one described above. Double Blind and Sequential Lineups have been adopted by different states throughout the nation. These different lineup procedures were designed to lessen the likelihood of a misidentification or police misconduct.

A Sequential Lineup is set up similarly as the investigatory lineup: the room, five (5) fillers and the suspect, but the victim/witness does not view all six (6) individuals at the same time. Each person is brought into the room alone, one at a time. This is a harder identification process, but it can mitigate misidentifications.

A Double Blind Lineup is the same as the investigatory lineup, but the investigators that are conducting the lineup do not know which person is the perpetrator as well as the victim/witness. In April 2001, the State of New Jersey became the first state in the Union to utilize the double blind lineup and photo array whenever practical (Cronin, Murphy, Spahr, Toliver & Weger, 2007, p. 44).

CI Cheat Sheet

Here is a quick formula reminder on when to use an array or a lineup:

NOT in custody = Array
IN custody = Lineup

Questions for Discussion and Review:

1. In order, name the three (3) types of eyewitness identification procedures employed by the police.

2. Should a suspect have an absolute right to counsel at an investigatory lineup? Why or why not?

3. If a suspect's lawyer requests to be at his client's lineup, how long do the police have to give him/her to arrive at the station house?

4. Should either a Sequential or Double Blind Lineup be mandated for all police department across the United States? Why or why not?

5. Can the police force a suspect into a lineup?

6. If a victim said, "I'm 99% sure it's #4," would that be a positive identification? Why or why not?

7. Why aren't eyewitness identification procedures used to identify a perpetrator that the victim knows?

8. How can the police prevent witness contamination?

9. Why do you think the police can't use a photo array if someone is in custody?

10. What is the minimum number of fillers that can be used in an array?

11. What is the minimum number of individuals that must stand in a lineup?

12. Which Amendment(s) of the U.S. Constitution deals with lawyers?

13. Which Amendment grants protection against impermissibly suggestive identification procedures?

14.   What are all of the rights which are protected under the 5th Amendment?

15.   Can the police use a photo of a "filler" that makes it stand out against the rest? Why or why not?

Chapter 7

Interview and Interrogation

"There are only two people in this world you should lie to, the police and your girlfriend."

— Jack Nicholson

The Liar's Puzzle

Why do people lie? The answer to this question is simpler than you think. From my own experience, human beings are taught at a very early age that there are good lies (white lies) and bad lies. But aren't they still lies? Of course they are. So it's alright to tell your aunt with a mustache that she looks good, so you don't hurt her feelings? In fact we even lie to ourselves! We also learn that lying is a way of escaping punishment. "Did you break the lamp because you were playing ball in the house?" "Yes, I did." Your response is then followed by either a smack or a "wait till your father gets home" threat. You say to yourself, "boy I'm never gonna admit to something like that again." Naturally, all future responses to "interrogations" by your parents will be full of denials followed by demands for proof. I can hear kids everywhere saying, "Hey Ma, you got that on videotape?"

Learning how to be a better liar doesn't end in childhood. By the time we are young adults we have begun to understand the technique of deception. This practice prepares us for marriage and the famous, "Does this make me look fat?" question. "You know it does, or you wouldn't have asked me in the first place." Could you even imagine what would happen if you said that? You would be sleeping with one eye open for sure! We lie to our parents, loved ones, friends and strangers. No one is immune to this phenomenon; some spouses would say they lie for survival reasons!

We begin to see how the pieces have developed and fallen into place in our lives. Lying is like putting a puzzle together. Some only have just the edges completed, some the middle, while others have the entire puzzle mastered. We encounter people who are very good liars and who lie for the sake of lying without even benefiting. Generally, there is a benefit of lying for most people. Some want out of a relationship, "It's not you, it's me," some want to get out of work, "I'm not feeling well today," and some don't want to go out with you, "I'm dyeing my hair tonight." In police work the stakes are much higher. People lie to stay out of jail, prison and in extreme cases the electric chair. They have nothing to lose and everything to gain by lying. It's up to you, the investigator, to identify lies and deception and somehow get to the truth of the matter. Easier said then done.

How does the Liar's Puzzle effect police work? Well, your first step to completing a regular puzzle was to dump all the pieces on the table, sort them by type: edge and interior pieces, and generally start with putting the edges together first. The liar does the same thing with the facts of the incident. They dump the facts in their head; separate the types of facts/lies (pieces) and starts with peripherals (edges) of the incident. Gradually, a skilled investigator asks the right questions, begins to push the individual to put the pieces of the puzzle (incident) together. This is why the technique of asking someone to tell the story backwards or to pick it up from the middle is so effective. Liars can't do it.

The two main ways individuals lie are by hiding and by making things up. Which one is worse? They are both forms of lying, but if it makes you feel better, much of hiding would fall under the "white lie" category. Lying by hiding is rather easy, because the individual is not actually telling any lies, he/she selectively tells you what you want or what they think you want to hear and leaves out the information that may implicate them. Hiding information is not lying you contend? Alright, then ask yourself this question, "If I told (fill in the blank with wife, husband, boss, detective, etc.) would I be in big trouble?" If the answer to this question is yes, you lied by hiding.

A "Puzzle" of someone who hides information has the edges done, most of the picture completed, but they are missing a few key pieces. Therefore, hiding is more difficult, but not impossible for an investigator to detect. Investigators must know the facts of the case and be familiar with each part of the investigation so they can detect if someone is hiding information from them.

An individual that hides information from an investigator may be a **CON** artist that:

Conceals
Omits
Not forthright

Making things up is a separate category. Someone that makes up information better have a good memory. Even a good memory pitted against a skilled investigator is no match. When someone falsifies, their "Puzzle," pieces are scattered all over the place, lacking structure, and therefore making it easier to uncover. The pieces simply do not fit.

An individual that makes things up may be an **ELF**, or one who:

Embellishes
Lies outright
Fabricates

A skilled investigator has to be a convincing liar also—fight fire with fire. An investigator is allowed to trick and deceive a suspect in order to obtain a confession as long as if the methods used could not coerce an innocent person to confess. Several court cases, most notably *Frazier v. Cupp* 394 U.S. 731 (1969), have rubber stamped the verbal allegation by law enforcement that evidence or statements exist to prove the suspect's guilt. For example, the courts have accepted informing a suspect that his/her fingerprints/DNA were/was found at a crime scene, or that the co-defendant implicated the other, when they did not or that a video surveillance tape existed depicting the suspect entering/leaving the location. Statements that make the suspect say to himself, "Do I call their bluff?"

For argument sake you cancel a night out with your girlfriend because you are not "feeling" well and therefore you are going to bed early. However, your intention is to go out to the sports pub with your friends to watch the football game. The next day she smugly asks, "how are you feeling?" "OK, I guess." "Are you sure?" That last question would leave you a little uneasy, no? Does she know something?

The grey area of deceit and trickery comes in the form of fabricating evidence. Appeals courts have given split decisions on the tactic of fabricating evidence in order to obtain a confession.

In the case, *State v. Cayward* 552 S.2d 971 (Florida 1989), the police presented a fabricated laboratory report specifically tying the suspect's DNA to a sexual assault and murder of a five year old girl. After seeing the report, the suspect confessed. The Florida Appeals Court decided that fabricated documents violate due process. In direct contrast to this decision, the Supreme Court of Nevada upheld the use of a fabricated laboratory report tying a suspect's DNA to a sexual assault in *Sheriff v. Bessey* 914 P.2d 618 (Nevada 1996). I would make an educated guess that the U.S. Supreme Court will eventually be asked to weigh in on this practice. Until they do, I believe that most police departments will avoid this tactic.

Conducting Interviews

"It is an old maxim of mine that when you have excluded the impossible, whatever remains, however, improbable, must be the truth."
— Sherlock Holmes (Sir Arthur Conan Doyle)

An investigator spends most of their time speaking with people. Even with the terrific advancements in the forensic sciences, especially with DNA, the need for human interaction is critical to the investigative process. Generally, when an investigator or reporter conducts an interview their goal is to develop information and answers to questions that they do not know. Keep this in mind, because when we get to interrogation, the goal changes. During an interrogation the investigator/reporter attempts to validate the information they already know. An interview is NOT an interrogation.

Conducting interviews is not an easy task for some individuals. If you are shy or introverted, you may have a tough time making it as an investigator because so much of what you do depends on your interactions with others. Interviewing is a skill that an investigator gets better at the more they do it. An investigator will learn what works and what doesn't and they also learn that the same techniques that they were successful with in the past are no guarantee that they will work with everybody. This is what makes interviewing so difficult. An investigator has to read a person, determine their level of comprehension and decide on what approach will work best all in the matter of seconds. Rarely will you ever get the chance to make a good first second impression.

If you ask investigators how they would define an interview, most would probably say, "A two-way conversation with an intention." The intention is to extract information. During an interview, the interviewer does a lot of listening and not so much talking. Interviews are non-custodial, which means no lawyers or Miranda Warnings are necessary. Interviews are not combative and should be conducted in a relaxed environment.

The key to **GREAT** interviewing is:

> **G**roundwork
> **R**apport Building
> **E**lucidation of Statements
> **A**ctive Listening
> **T**he Assessment

Groundwork

Before conducting interviews, investigators must know what happened. For example, shortly after arriving at a scene of a major incident, the investigators should be gathered together by the investigator supervisor and the case investigator. Additional investigators who arrive at the scene play a support role. They must be brought up to speed regarding evidence that was found, who the victim was and what were the circumstances surrounding the crime. Investigators should be thinking about the type of questions they want to ask, not only to the citizens but to the case investigator as well.

If time permits, computer checks should be done on the suspect and the building/house the investigators will be canvassing. "Running" the location in computer databases can provide information such as: residents, persons wanted on warrants or other crimes, and parolees. The most important reason to conduct computer checks is for officer safety. I personally, would want to know that the door I was about to knock on, may be the residence of someone that is wanted for a crime. Armed with this information, the investigator can now start to canvass (See Chapter 5). The investigative canvass is a series of interviews conducted over a short period of time. The locations canvassed and the information obtained must be properly documented on an investigative report or it may be lost forever.

Rapport Building

Building rapport is one of the most important, if not thee most important aspect of conducting interviews. Building rapport is not as easy as it sounds. There are four (4) types of people an investigator will encounter during police/public interviews: (1) those who hate the police, (2) those who are scared of the police, (3) those who distrust the police and (4) those who like the police. An investigator has one strike against them before knocking on the door, so rapport building is extremely important to win over the individual's co-operation. Looking the part is also important. A well dressed investigator engenders a level of respect as well as presenting a professional image. In my experience, people are more willing to open up to a "suit" then to the uniforms.

Rapport building is an attempt by the interviewer to identify common ground between them and the interviewee. It may be a quick acknowledgment of a sports team shirt, or photos of children or a boat in the driveway. Anything to get the "two-way conversation" started. This only works if the investigator properly introduces themselves and makes a quick statement as to why they are there. "Hi, sir/ma'am, my name is Detective Magpie from the ABC Police. I am here seeking information about the incident that occurred a few hours ago. Do you mind if I come in?" If you noticed in this example opening statement by the investigator, he didn't request information as soon as the person answered the door. This is done for one reason, some people do not want to be seen talking to the police in public. It may not be good for their health or "street cred." People may be reluctant to provide information based on where you are standing and not so much as what you say. The environment can also play a role in obtaining information. Also, Detective Magpie referred to the situation as an incident and not what it really is, a murder, rape, robbery etc. This technique downplays the severity of the situation and may put the person at ease. Keeping people comfortable about the topic can never hurt you.

What you say is important, but sometimes not as important as how you say it. A negative attitude or disinterested questions may turn the person off and send you packing. If the investigator is rude, discourteous or talks down to the interviewee, they will wind up with nothing. This defeats the entire goal of an investigator: to obtain information and evidence to identify perpetrators (Chapter 1). Remember the old adage, "You get more flies with honey, then you do with vinegar."

Elucidation of Statements

To elucidate is to make clear or clarify. Investigators use a series of open-ended and closed-ended questions to extract information from people. An open-ended question elicits a story from the individual. "Tell me what happened?" would be an example of an open-ended question. Here the investigator is attempting to get a story. Interviews should be started with a series of open ended questions. Open ended questions cannot be answered with a simple, "yes" or "no" and therefore provide more information to work with. Open ended questions also allow the investigator to develop a baseline on how the interviewee reacts under questioning. Do they seem comfortable or uncomfortable with the topic or specific question? Are they able to talk about certain parts of the event without difficulty and then other parts exhibit signs of distress? Do they answer some questions quickly and then stutter and stammer when pressed for specific information?

A closed ended question attempts to establish facts and/or lock a person into a statement. "What time did you get home last night?" "Where you home last night?" "Do you know Mary Smith?" are all examples of closed-ended questions. A closed ended question can be answered with a simple yes, no or one word answer. Unlike the open ended questions, a closed ended questions look to elicit specific details of the event.

> **CI Tip Sheet**
>
> Just remember the following:
>
> Open Ended = Overview of the event - a story
> Closed Ended = Specifics

Before ending an interview, the investigator should paraphrase statements made by the individual to ensure accuracy and for clarification. This provides the interviewer a chance to check his/her facts and to lock a person into their statement. This is important because your witness may develop "amnesia" or change their story once they enter the courtroom. The prosecutor should be able to "refresh" their memory from a well prepared and documented report.

Some jurisdictions require the police to audiotape and video record all interviews and interrogations. Even though taping can cause an administrative nightmare for the police, an interview on tape can prove that the statement was not coerced from the individual. This can be very damaging to the perpetrator. Civil Libertarians have been fighting for this a long time and I don't know why. They claim that it prevents the police from coercing confessions, but I think about how damaging a confession on video tape would be. There is nothing for a defense attorney to challenge or could use to plant the seed in a jury's mind about reasonable doubt. They just watched the perpetrator admit to the crime!

Investigators must avoid using foul language, police jargon or street language and the use of certain types of questions. Questions from **UCLA** must never be used by an investigator:

Unclear
Compound
Leading
Any question or statement that could disclose investigative
    information

Unclear

An unclear question creates confusion for the interviewee because it is poorly constructed. "When you arrived home the day after yesterday and met your assailant, how did you know that he was your assailant and that he was about to attack you?" Huh?

Compound

A compound question should never be used because the interviewer asks at least two questions at the same time. More than likely, the interviewee will answer only the last question. "What time did you come home last night and what did you see?" Ask one question at a time, get your answer, then move onto the next one. In the preceding example, the time the person arrived home may be the most important question!

Leading

A leading question "leads" the interviewee to the answer or provides the answer. "He was driving a white Chevy, right?" "Did Mark do this to you?" Instead, the questions should have been asked this way, "What color was the car he was driving?" Get your answer, and then ask, "Who gave you the black eye?"

Any question or statement that could disclose investigative information

The investigator must be careful not to disclose investigative information that may be detrimental to the case when speaking with potential witnesses and suspects. Rarely will the police disclose all of the facts surrounding the case. Remember an interview was defined as a two-way street, so there is a chance that the investigator may leak information inadvertently. The police must "hold some things back" so that they can determine who is telling the truth and who is not. For instance, a "suspect" enters the stationhouse and claims he was the guy who killed the female jogger in the park. Depending on the situation, a case like this will garner a tremendous amount of media, so the police may withhold the cause of death. An investigator will take the person to an interview room, of course read him his Miranda Warnings (more on this in Conducting Interrogations) and ask some questions. After obtaining the man's pedigree information, the investigator may test the "confessor" right from the start, "How did you kill her?" "I strangled her." The investigator would then probably stand up, open the door to the interview room and say, "Next!"

Active Listening

If you have ever been told, "You never listen to me!" your spouse is probably right. An investigator has to listen and weigh every word used. An individual may make an incriminating statement or provide information that they shouldn't have, but only if the investigator is listening attentively will they hear it. The individual may choose words that will lead to additional follow up questions or make an inadvertent slip of the tongue. For example, investigators are conducting a canvass with an upstairs neighbor about a homicide that occurred in the building. The investigator asks, "Did you hear anything last night?" "I heard a scream and said to myself, that's Jimmy." There is an inadvertent slip. I personally wouldn't jump on it right away. I would save it for the right moment and ask, "Why did you think it was Jimmy?" or "How did you know it was Jimmy?"

The investigator must fight the urge to interrupt the person when they are speaking. This is known as breaking the stream of consciousness. Have you ever had a great dream, where everything was going perfect or you were having a good time and then the phone rings? You try and find that exact place in your bed, fluff your pillow just right and what happens? Nothing. You can never regain that stream of consciousness. The same thing happens to people who are interrupted in the middle of their story. Let them speak, jot down notes and when they are done, now elucidate (clarify) their statements.

Taking notes is an important part of the listening process. The notes provide a chance to ensure accuracy and completeness. When two investigators are present for an interview, only one will do the talking and the other will take notes. This decision should be made prior to conducting the interview. The general rule is that the case investigator will conduct both the interview(s) and interrogation(s) if practical. This is a good rule to follow because it makes it easier to testify in court when only one investigator conducted the interviews.

CI Tip Sheet

A quick guideline for note taking and to sum up the interviewing process is to catch a **LIAR**:

Listen Attentively
Intervene only if the interviewee loses focus
Add or correct information as needed
Review the notes with the interviewee before leaving

Remember, all notes taken must be preserved as "Rosario Material" (*People v. Rosario* 9 NY2d. 286 (1961)) in many jurisdictions. To be on the safe side, investigators should be in the habit of saving and securing all notes in the case folder.

The Assessment

The assessment or evaluation is a self-critique conducted by the interviewer regarding their interview. It is a very important step. An assessment can prevent mistakes in the future and the techniques that were discovered can be used to train other investigators. The investigator must be honest with themselves. Did they ask the right questions? Would they have done something different? What worked what didn't work? Was it easier or harder than first thought and why? These questions are a good starting point in the self evaluation process. In order for the assessment to be successful, the investigator must be honest with their own self. Self-evaluation is often difficult.

Preventing Interview Contamination

An investigator has the difficult task of ensuring that the interview is not contaminated. Contamination can occur many ways but the worst kind of contamination occurs when witnesses/victims talk to one another. An investigator must keep witnesses/victims separated at all costs! Other contamination issues are distractions like phones ringing, babies crying, and televisions playing. An investigator has to be careful when they ask the homeowner to lower the radio/ TV or put the children in another room. Remember, you are a guest that has a purpose.

Cell phone usage presents an even bigger problem. Witnesses/victims should be strongly encouraged not to use their phones until all of the interviews are completed. If the resources exist, a uniformed police officer should stay with each victim/witness to help prevent contamination. Remember, they all do not have to be in the same room to talk with one another.

Conducting Interrogations

> *"If you can't get them to tell you the truth, get them to tell you lies."*
>
> — Joseph L. Giacalone

You often hear this topic called the "Art of Interrogation." In a way, it is an accurate depiction of the process as long as the student understands that even famous painters started out drawing stick figures. I can't stress the fact enough that the only way to get good at interrogating suspects is by doing it. You are going to make mistakes and you will fail in achieving your goal (a confession), but you will also obtain some confessions even when you were not at your very best. Conducting interrogations is similar to professional sports. Sometimes things will go your way and sometimes they won't. It all evens out in the end.

Television has taken advantage of the "Art of Interrogation" and introduced the highly popular show, *The Closer* on TNT. All that I can tell you is that there are no specialists who come in at the end of your interrogation and obtain the confession for you. If you have been paying attention so far, you would see that a "closer" would be at a huge disadvantage in an interrogation room because they could not possibly know all of the requisite information on the case. Television is fantasy and entertainment, that's all.

Ideally, the last step of every criminal investigation should be the interrogation. The investigator must find out all of the available information regarding the case so that he/she would know if a suspect is corroborating what the police already know or that they are lying. An interrogation is not like conducting an interview. An interrogation is custodial, adversarial in nature and the goal is to develop a certainty of guilt. Even with advances in DNA and physical evidence to aid in establishing guilt, the words from the perpetrator's own mouth are usually what sinks them. An oral, written or recorded confession is powerful evidence.

CI Tip Sheet

We interview victims and witnesses
We interrogate suspects/perpetrators.

We are going to build on the keys to **GREAT** Interviewing that we learned from conducting interviews, by carrying those principles over into the interrogation room. For instance, the interrogator must employ active listening in order to hear what is being said or not said and be able to follow up and press for answers. The main difference between an interview and an interrogation is the custodial nature of the event. By the time an investigator is ready to interrogate, a suspect's guilt has been reasonably established from the physical evidence, victim/witness statements and or identifications. Therefore, before we learn about the basics of interrogation techniques, the student must understand the legal implications and/or ramifications of custodial interrogation.

Custodial interrogation is when the police have a person under arrest (they are no longer free to leave) and they are going to ask the questions that are narrowly related to the event. Here is a question for the reader, "do you believe that once you are under arrest, the police must read the Miranda Warnings to you?" If you said yes to that question, you are a victim of television. Only in Hollywood do they start with, "You have the right to remain silent..." as soon as the cuffs are slapped on. In reality, when the cuffs go on, those deep, dramatic words are rarely used. The police do not have to read a suspect their Miranda Warnings unless that have custody and they are going to interrogate (Giacalone, Writing.com 2004). Not every perpetrator will be interrogated.

CI Tip Sheet

Here is a quick math formula to help you remember when the
police must read the Miranda Warnings:

CUSTODY + INTERROGATION = MIRANDA

Who was this guy Miranda anyway? Ernesto Miranda was
arrested in the state of Arizona in 1963, where he confessed
to the kidnapping and raping of a mildly retarded teenager.
Miranda did not know that he had a right to remain silent, a
right that came about from a strict interpretation of the Fifth
Amendment to the Constitution when he signed his written
statement. His conviction for the crime, partially based on his
confession, was overturned and Ernesto was granted a new
trial .

Supreme Court Justice Earl Warren presented the
following procedural Fifth Amendment safeguards for future
custodial interrogations:

> *"The person in custody must, prior to interrogation, be*
> *clearly informed that he has the right to remain silent,*
> *and that anything he says will be used against him in*
> *court; he must be clearly informed that he has the right*
> *to consult with a lawyer and to have the lawyer with*
> *him during interrogation, and that, if he is indigent, a*
> *lawyer will be appointed to represent him."* (*Miranda v.*
> *Arizona* 384 U.S. 436 (1966)).

The improperly obtained confession could not be used
against him in the re-trial. His girlfriend's testimony, however,
could be used. He was convicted for the second time. Miranda
served several years in prison for his horrific crime; he was
subsequently released back into society. Justice however,
would not be denied. In 1976, Miranda was stabbed to death
during a bar fight. When the police arrested a suspect for the
murder, the accused refused to make incriminating
statements. Without the proper identification, the suspect was
released. The murder was never solved because this suspect
invoked his right to remain silent. There's irony for you.

The Miranda decision made it mandatory that law enforcement officers across the United States read the Miranda

Warnings to any individual in *police custody that will be questioned.* If not, any incriminating statements will be inadmissible. The police should read the Miranda Warnings from a card word-for-word, but may use simple direct language if the situation calls for it. However, the investigator must document how and why he/she used other language to explain the individual's Miranda Warnings.

The Miranda decision has been applauded by civil libertarians and disputed by crime control advocates since it happened. Over the years, like we saw with search and seizure, exceptions to the "rule" have been carved out from the Miranda decision. Crime control advocates have applauded. Generally, these exceptions have been made to protect the lives of citizens and the police.

In the case *Rhode Island v. Innis* 446 US 291 (1980), any spontaneous utterance or statement made by a defendant in custody can be incriminating as long as it was not in response to a question posed by the police. For example, the police arrest a suspect for murdering his wife and put him in the interrogation room. The police are preparing a strategy for the interrogation when the suspect says, "I want my lawyer." The police stop planning the interrogation and start with the booking process. During fingerprinting, the suspect says to the investigator, "She was cheating on me. I did what I had to do. I killed her." This statement is a confession or a direct acknowledgement of guilt. It will be used against the suspect in the court of law, even though he previously invoked his right to counsel.

In the case, *New York v. Quarles* 467 US 649 (1984), we see the "public safety" exception. This decision allows law enforcement to question a suspect in custody without the benefit of Miranda when an exigent circumstance exists which require protection of the public; in this case a gun hidden in a grocery store (Giacalone, Writing.com (2004).

Does the Right to Counsel attach during other situations other than custodial interrogation? Yes. When the defendant's lawyer has a **CAR**:

Contacted by lawyer
Accusatory instrument has been filed
Retains a lawyer for the matter under investigation

Contacted by lawyer

If a lawyer contacts the police looking for their client, the right to counsel attaches. All interrogations must stop unless the lawyer is present. This presents a problem for big police departments because the lawyer doesn't even have to know what precinct his/her client is in. If the lawyer told one cop in the department, he told everybody. It would be incumbent upon the precinct where the call was made to send out a message to all of the other commands to notify them that this person is represented by counsel and that all questioning must cease.

Accusatory instrument has been filed

If an indictment (True Bill) has been handed down or an arrest warrant has been issued, an absolute right to counsel comes attached with it. This is the reason why investigators don't like obtaining arrest warrants—they can't speak to the suspect about the case unless their lawyer is present.

Retains a lawyer for the matter under investigation

If a suspect is not in custody and has retained a lawyer for the particular matter under investigation and the police are aware of it, they cannot talk to him about that particular case. But, since he is not in custody, the police can talk to him about an unrelated matter without his lawyer being present. For instance, Johnny Jones was arrested for a robbery and is currently on bail. No matter if Johnny hired a lawyer or not, he was provided one free of charge at his arraignment. Johnny is released on his own recognizance and given another court date to show up. The police want to question Johnny about a murder they think he was involved in. Can they talk to him about the murder without his lawyer present? Yes. Would the answer change if he is in custody still on the robbery? Yes. If you are in custody and awaiting trial, the police cannot talk to you about any case, related or not unless your lawyer is present.

CI Tip Sheet

When investigators can speak to suspects that have lawyers:

Not in Jail on the related crime — No
Not in Jail on an unrelated crime — Yes
In Jail on an unrelated crime or not — No

It is difficult to defend the argument that the police "didn't know he had a lawyer" because if the investigator conducted the proper background checks, he would have found out. If an investigator interviews or interrogates any suspect in direct violation of the 5th Amendment, any information received will be inadmissible.

You may have never thought of it this way, but the oldest recorded interrogation is the Bible story of Adam and Eve. Adam and Eve's story contains valuable lessons for student interrogators:

- A separation of "co-conspirators" before questioning
- The use of open and closed ended questions
- The use of base line questions to develop a normal pattern of answers
- The "Interrogator" knew the answers to the questions
  o   He asked to test truthfulness
- The "Interrogator" used the suspect's non-verbal body language to decipher uneasiness with certain questions
- The "Interrogator" did not reveal information about the investigation to the suspects
- The suspects ultimately lied
  o   Used emphatic denials at first
  o   Finger pointing and alibi crafting to obfuscate the truth
- The "Interrogator" used questions and their answers to "get them" off their denials and to the truth
- The case ended in punishment

When the heat is on in the interrogation room, turn up the **AC**! The investigator's goal in an interrogation is to obtain either an **A**dmission or a **C**onfession. Ideally, a confession is the desired result.

An admission is a statement that self-incriminates, but falls short of owning up to committing the act. "I was there, but I didn't kill him." An **admission** can open the door to a confession. Further development of the admission may lead to the name of the perpetrator (if not the person you are interrogating). An admission could be used to charge someone for a crime, so it holds a tremendous amount of weight in an investigation. The idea is to get the person talking.

In cases where there were multiple perpetrators, the admission will more than likely be used as testimony against the main perpetrator. A thorough investigation can yield an admission by confronting the suspect with evidence of his/her whereabouts. For instance, video surveillance footage recovered from a canvass showing the suspect inside of the grocery store around the time of the murder, or cell phone records placing them in the area at a particular time.

A **confession** is when an individual acknowledges their guilt by incriminating oneself as the perpetrator of a crime. "Yes, I shot her." This is of course, the ultimate goal of an interrogation, but not always possible. Sometimes you have to settle for an admission and develop the rest of the case around that by destroying the suspect's alibi, obtaining witness statements and recovering physical evidence.

The question is how do we find our way to the truth? You get there by doing what you do when you go someplace for the first time: you look it up on a map, or online, or you ask someone else who has already been there. You need a road map for where you are going because each interrogation is like a road trip that involves lots of traffic jams, tie ups and u-turns. Sometimes, when things aren't going well, you have to get off the main road and take the back streets or a dirt road to get to where you have to be. It may be long and rough, but the goal is the same, arrive at the desired destination.

Most things begin with a planning and preparation phase before anything else. An interrogation is no different. The case investigator must thoroughly review the case and speak with other investigators that helped obtain information from canvasses. Sometimes, the case investigator is not the best choice to conduct the interrogation. There may be another investigator who has more experience or that may have struck up a good rapport with the suspect, an essential element of any interview or interrogation. This decision will ultimately be made by the investigator supervisor, unless a previous agreement has been reached. However, other factors such as culture and gender issues could come into play such as the nature of the crime. For instance, an individual has a long history of abuse on women and now he is the prime suspect in the brutal murder of his wife. The investigating supervisor may decide to have a male officer conduct the interview. But it may work to your advantage as well. Would a female investigator make the suspect even more arrogant and cocky that he may slip?

In cases with multiple perpetrators the decision has to be made on who should be interrogated first. The decision can be based on at least three (3) choices:

(1) The individual who has the most to lose
(2) The weakest link
(3) The person who has never been to prison before.

(1) The person, who may be willing to "roll over" on the others to save their own skin when in a tough spot, may be the first choice. A three time loser or someone who just violated their parole are examples of individuals who have the most to lose.
(2) The weakest link can be described with the following example: three suspects are put in a cell and two go right to sleep and
(3) the individual who is new to the arrest process and hanging on the cell bars may be a good starting point.

As you can see, planning and preparation are important pre-requisites to any investigation.

An investigator must ensure that their plan has an **EKG**:

Environmental/setting considerations
Knowledge of how and why
Ground work on all parties involved

Environmental/setting considerations

Where the interrogation takes place plays an important role in obtaining a confession or admission. There is no argument that the location is in the advantage of the police. The most important factor when preparing and planning an interview is officer safety. A complete and thorough search of the suspect must be made before they are put in the interview room, AKA "The Box." Anything that could aid in escape or cause injury must be removed from the individual. In addition, any electronic devices should also be removed. Investigators should never be armed in the interview room.

The room should be small, free from distractions (phones, newspapers, etc.), with no wanted posters on the walls and be equipped with a one way mirror. Are you asking, why no wanted posters? Think about it for a moment. You are sitting in the interview room and you know what you did or didn't do. You are waiting for the investigators to come back into the room. You may be nervous and or bored. Your eyes start to dart around the room. Now you are looking at all of these photos of persons wanted for all types of heinous crimes. You start to think about the predicament you got yourself into. You'd probably dig your heels in and fight for your freedom. No?

The room should contain three (3) chairs, two (2) for the investigators and one (1) for the suspect and a small table that should be off to the side. One of the investigators will play the role of note taker (Investigator #2) and will not participate in the interrogation unless asked to by Investigator #1 (Figure 7.1).

Figure 7.1

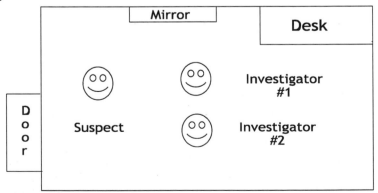

If you examine Figure 7.1 carefully, you should have noticed three (3) things that aren't the norm for interrogation rooms:

(1) the suspect has his/her back to the door,
(2) the desk is off to the side and
(3) that the suspect is not looking into the mirror.

1. There are two (2) reasons why you don't want the suspect looking at the door. First, it is easier for another investigator to grab your attention when warranted, but most importantly the suspect isn't staring at the exist thinking, "That's my way out!" The investigator has to be concerned about an escape attempt as well as a physical assault. When suspects get desperate they resort to desperate measures.

2. A desk between the suspect and the investigators is a barrier that benefits the suspect. It is something that they can "hide" behind. It also prevents the investigators from observing and identifying any non-verbal body cues given off by the suspect. Whenever possible, the desk should be pushed off to the side. Also, being close to the suspect causes them stress and anxiety. The closer the investigator moves in the more uncomfortable it is for the suspect. Moving closer to a suspect is done gradually in stages as the investigator builds the case against the suspect. It gives the "we're closing in on you" feeling. However, if the investigator moves in to quickly, the suspect may shut down.

3. You don't want the suspect looking into the mirror either. He/she may suspect that there is someone on the other side watching and listening, especially when they are in the room alone. Also, over time those mirrors lose their sheen and you can see through them. You would never want the suspect to see the complainant right through the glass.

Knowledge of how and why

The investigator must know every investigative step taken and every fact that has been obtained. They will speak to other investigators, medical examiners, victims, witnesses and review lab reports and crime scene photos. This is an effort to ensure thoroughness, accuracy and allow the investigator to establish the credibility of the investigation to the suspect. During the course of the interrogation the investigator will drop "hints" on the quality of the investigation and the amount of information that the police already know. The investigator may be looking to find a few of the pieces of the puzzle that are missing and address the elements of **MOM** (**M**eans, **O**pportunity and **M**otive).

The investigator has to be able to ask the right questions in order to "kill" the eventual denial and/or alibi. Like the villain in the James Bond movies, the investigator has to understand that the suspect is going drop **OIL** to evade telling the truth to the police:

Omit
Impede
Lie

The only way an investigator can overcome this is to make sure that they are prepared.

Knowledge of the how and why of the case also helps in vetting out "confessors" and "witnesses" that do not seem credible. This happens more times than you think, especially in high profile media cases. For example, the victim was bound, gagged and stabbed several times with an ice pick. The next morning an individual enters the stationhouse and turns himself in claiming to be the murderer. The investigator must treat every person who confesses as the perpetrator and will read him Miranda. Since this person has already "confessed" to the crime, the investigator may jump right to the incident after a few brief preliminary questions. "How did you kill her?" "I shot her." "Thank you for your time."

Ground work on all parties involved

Knowing who you are dealing with can give the investigator some insight on how to interrogate them. The individual's age, education level, job and experience with the criminal justice system are factors that must be considered before any interrogation begins. An investigator cannot interrogate an individual that has a rap sheet as long as his arm the same way he/she would a first time offender. As previously stated, the investigator will decide on whom to speak with first in a multiple suspect case based on their background.

The ground work includes more than past interactions with the police, but information of the suspect's whereabouts prior to and after the crime. This can play a pivotal role in the investigation. It provides critical time frames for the investigator to prove/disprove alibis and statements. For example, identifying the approximate location of an individual via a subpoena of their cell phone GPS coordinates. It's hard to explain that you weren't "there," when your phone puts you there. To avoid the retort, "I lent me phone to a friend," I would have asked him if he had his phone with him or did he make any calls prior to telling him about the subpoena so I could lock him down into his statement. An investigative step like this takes time to develop and this is why you always want to interrogate last.

The Interrogation Process

The investigator is now at the crossroads on when and where to start. Getting ready to conduct an interrogation is very similar to getting ready to act in a play. It's show time. You've memorized your lines, prepared the "stage," your supporting cast is in place and you're now ready to perform. The investigator will walk into the room and introduce themselves if it wasn't done already. Remember, there is custody and interrogation, what do we need? Right. The investigator will read and/or explain the Miranda Warnings to the suspect. If the suspect wishes to answer questions, the investigator will have them initial each line of the Miranda Warnings and sign a department form. A refusal to initial the paper or sign their name does not invoke the right to counsel. In order to obtain a valid waiver of one's rights, the individual must do so Voluntarily, Intelligently and Knowingly. Silence can never be construed as consent.

CI Tip Sheet

In order to have a valid waiver for conducting a search without a warrant or to waive Miranda it must be given:

Voluntarily
Intelligently
Knowingly

What can make a waiver of one's Miranda Rights *invalid?*

PAD can make a waiver invalid:

Promises or threats
  o   Promises of time off or other court consideration (only the ADA can do this!)
  o   Threats to deport them or their family
  o   Threats to arrest other family members

Any use of force to get the confession (self explanatory)

Denial of essential accommodations
  o   Food, bathroom, breaks, sleep

Remember, in an interrogation, the investigator will do most of the talking. There are four (4) parts of an interrogation that the student investigator can use as their **ROAD** map to help find their way to the truth:

Reduce resistance
Obtain an admission
Admission development
Documented on paper

Reduce resistance

As stated earlier, an interrogation is adversarial in nature, so resistance will be evident from the very beginning. Do you think someone is really going to say, "Hi detective, I know you have to go to your kids softball game, so I'll make this quick.

Yes, I shot Johnny Jones because he encroached on my drug dealing operation. Please lock me up and send me to jail the rest of my life. If you give me a piece of paper I'll be more than happy to write it all out for you." Sounds ridiculous right? The stakes are very high for the suspect. He/she could go to jail the rest of their lives. As one would surmise, resistance will be the strongest at the very beginning of the interrogation, so an investigator must be careful not to push too hard. Remember, an interrogation is not a conversation. You start by accusing the suspect of a heinous crime! How do you think they are going to react?

Resistance comes in the form of denials. There are two (2) types of denials: the emphatic denial and the explanatory denial. An emphatic denial is one where the suspect will refuse any knowledge or participation in the crime. "I don't know what you are talking about. I wasn't there," or the famous, "It wasn't me." An explanatory denial is one where the suspect will offer up an excuse why they couldn't be involved. "I come from a very religious family. My mother always made sure we went to church" (Zulawski & Wicklander, 2001, p. 343-358). "I'm married, why would I have sex with that girl?"

Denials can develop because the suspect wants some **PIE**:

Past experience with the Criminal Justice System
Interrogator's lack of experience, poor choice of approach and/or plan of attack
Environment is not conducive for interrogation purposes - timing, location, distractions

It is the investigator's job to identify who is telling the truth and who is lying. It is not that easy to do. If it were, we'd all be in trouble! How do people act, how do they talk when they lie? Access to videos and newscasts over the Internet allows the student to train themselves to detect lies. Learn from those who have already done it and got caught. Choose from anyone that we know for a fact lied and study their before and after statements as well as their non-verbal body language, such as: Richard Nixon, Bill Clinton, Mark Hacking,

Susan Smith, Alex Rodriguez or Scott Peterson to name a few. Listen to what they said and how they said or didn't say it. Study the words they chose and their body language. An investigator in training could learn a lot from these simple clips.

The strength of a denial is also important to the astute investigator. They can come in two strengths: strong and weak. Bill Clinton's infamous speech to the American people would be a great example of a strong denial:

> *"I want to say one thing to the American people. I want you to listen to me I'm going to say this again. I did not have sexual relations with that woman. Miss Lewinsky. I never told anybody to lie, not a single time, never. These allegations are false and I need to go back to work for the American people. Thank you." (YouTube, posted on August 30, 2006).*

We now know that everything he said, with the exception of thank you, was a lie. The idea behind using a strong denial is to shut the accuser down, which is exactly what the President was able to do. It can be very effective against anyone that is not sure of themselves. I want the student to play the video over and over again and try to identify any signs of deception. They may not be recognizable at first, but you can pick them up as you train your eyes and ears to see and hear the lies. The ironic part is if you can find the video for the Nixon "Watergate" speech, it is eerily similar to Bill Clinton's "Monicagate" speech.

A weak denial is one that is given rather sheepishly. For example, listen to baseball superstar Alex Rodriguez's denial to Katie Couric about the use of performance enhancing drugs (Gaines, 2009).

KC: "For the record, did you ever use steroids, human growth hormone or any other performance enhancing substance?"

AR: "No."

KC: "Have you ever been tempted to use any of those things?"

AR: slight pause and head shake, "No."

KC: "You never felt like, this guy is doing it. Maybe I should look into this too. He's getting better numbers, playing better ball?"

AR: "I never felt overmatched on the baseball field. I always been in a very strong, dominate position. And I felt if I did my work since I've done since I was, ahh, you know a rookie back in Seattle. I didn't have a problem competing at any level, so, uh, no."

You can see the difference in the tone of voice, the inflection in the voice, the calmness and the words chosen as compared to Clinton's strong denial. In addition, he does not answer the question. He stalls for time which is another clue that the person may not be telling the truth. There are a few instances where the viewer can pick up changes in facial expressions when certain questions are asked, see if you can find them (see References for the link).

The question becomes, "How does the investigator overcome a denial?" The investigator doesn't want this to turn into a schoolyard argument: "Did not," "Did to," "Did not," Did to," etc. An investigator can combat denials by presenting alternatives or excuses on why the person did the crime. An investigator can gain the advantage over the suspect by offering them a way out by having the suspect think what they did was alright. It is an opportunity for the suspect to save face. Excuses can take many forms, but it is always a good idea to a make a **BID** for an admission/confession using one of these:

Blame game
Increase feelings of guilt or shame
Diminish the seriousness of the crime

Other excuses do exist, but these are probably the most popular ones employed by investigators. If you haven't noticed yet, an investigator must be good at the lying game too!

Blame game

Have you ever noticed that when someone gets involved in a car accident it is **NEVER** their fault? It is *always* the other guy's fault. Individuals like to fix blame and do so quickly. For this reason, I believe there is no better way to get the perpetrator to feel okay about what they have done than to play the "blame game." The failure to take responsibility for one's actions has fueled the need for using the blame game. When an investigator places blame squarely on the shoulders of the victim, it allows the suspect to relax and make them feel better at the moment. It sounds harsh, but you don't actually believe or feel what you are saying. The investigator lies to the suspect in order to get them to open up about the event. For instance, in a rape case, an investigator can cast blame on the victim with any of the following questions or statements:

- "I know the victim came on to you, how could she resist a good looking guy like you? You didn't do anything that any ordinary guy wouldn't have done."
- "Listen. I get it. You spent a lot of money on dinner and you expected something in return. I know I would. It's a guy thing."
- "I saw that dress she was wearing. I wouldn't be able to control my urges either."
- "The way she was dressed, she as asking for it."

In a murder investigation an investigator could use any of the following:

- "We have thoroughly investigated this case and we discovered that you were only defending yourself. He (insert victim's name) would still be alive today if he hadn't attacked you first."
- "If I came home and found my spouse in bed with someone else, I would have stabbed them to death too. Their actions and lack of respect for you in your own bed drove you to do it."

As sick as these statements/questions sound, the idea is to get the suspect to talk carelessly about the event. This is when you will find out if you established a good rapport with the individual. If the suspect feels he/she has to justify their actions then they will buy into the "blame game."

Increase feelings of guilt or shame

Religion and your mother are the greatest causes for feelings of guilt and shame. No one in my opinion does it better! Cultural or religious issues are easy to develop.

- "Sam, Margaret is a very devout Catholic girl. She was saving herself for marriage. Now her life and her plans have totally changed by this event."

- "Fred. Do you know how upset your mom is right now? She's totally heartbroken. But I know she raised you to do the right thing. My mom is just like yours and she would want me to come clean too."

- "Who am I to pass judgment on you? I haven't done everything right in my life either."

- "Listen. I know how it is. I wasn't always a cop you know."

Diminish the seriousness of the crime

When you diminish the seriousness of the crime, you are providing an open door for the suspect to step in and explain their actions. The suspect believes that a diminished crime will equal diminished time. Shakespeare once said, "A rose by any other name is still a rose." It doesn't matter what words you use to diminish the crime. It is what it is. The investigator must be careful using the stark words of murder, rape, robbed, beat etc. to the suspect, especially when attempting to diminish the event. When you read the following statements pay close attention to the italicized words and phrases.

- "I know you had *consensual intercourse* with that young girl. You didn't force her like she claims."

- "You're not as *bad* as (fill in the blank) that did XY and Z."

- "When your wife got *hurt*, where were you standing?"

- "We know you got caught up *in this whole thing* and that you had nothing to do with planning the incident. But, someone *died*."

- "It was an *accident*. It could have happened to any one of us."

Obtain an admission

The investigator is now at the stage where the suspect has been thoroughly convinced about the quality of the investigation and about the facts that the police have already laid out. An admission confirms the interrogator's assertion that the suspect was involved when they obtain one. It is an acknowledgement of their involvement in the incident. The investigator has listened to the **OIL** (**O**mit, **I**mpede, **L**ie) the suspect has dropped so far and has digested the suspect's alibi. The suspect has been presented excuses for their behavior and is now primed for the investigator to move in.

Obtaining an admission can be a lengthy affair. Is there any limit on how long you can interrogate somebody? The answer is no, as long as the person was given adequate bathroom breaks, something to eat and time to rest. These events must be documented on a department form (Figure 7.2), an investigator's report and if possible written in the suspect's final statement (see Documented on paper below). It would be extremely difficult for the suspect's attorney to mount a defense that the police coerced the confession from his client.

Figure 7.2

Person Interviewed: _____   Date: _____
Case # _____

TIME		LOCATION	OFFICERS PRESENT	ACTIVITY
FROM	TO			
1200	1215	54 Squad - Interview Room	None	Alone
1215	1315	do	Giacalone & Weaver	Rights & Interview
1315	1345	do	Giacalone	Bathroom / Refused food
1345	1500	do	Giacalone & Weaver	Interview / Confession
1500	1600	do	Alone	Lunch
1600	1630	do	Sister: Joy Alleto	Chatting
1630	1700	do	Giacalone & Weaver	Written Statement
1700	1715	do	Alone	None
1715		Removal to Central Booking	Giacalone & Weaver	

The investigator will now begin to poke holes in the suspect's story. For example, the suspect denies ever being at the location. Getting them to come off of their denial and into an admission could be as simple as showing them a still photo taken from a video surveillance camera of the suspect at the scene. Here is another example: The investigator is questioning a suspect about a rape and asks, "Do you know Mary Jane?" "I don't know the girl." "Have you ever had intercourse with Mary Jane?" "What's the matter with you man? I told you, I don't know her!" The investigator pulls a sheet of paper from the case folder and hands it to the suspect. "Do you know what this is?" "No, what is it?" "That (insert suspect's name), is a DNA report from the medical examiner's office. I want you to pay special attention to the second paragraph. Can you explain to me how your DNA ended up inside of the victim?" Then the Oh S*%$ light bulb goes off. "Ohhhhhhh, that Mary Jane."

An investigator obtains an admission by knowing the case, having the facts, crafting the right questions and choosing the right moments to drop them on the suspect. If you think that you have enough information, dig deeper! When investigators are ill prepared or lack the experience terrible things can happen to the case. Here is a small example of how not to conduct an interrogation. The following snippet was extracted from the O.J. Simpson statement (November 29, 1994 issue of STAR Magazine):

Det. Vannatter: *"So what time do you think you got back home, actually physically got home?"*

Simpson: *"Seven-something."*

Det. Vannatter: *"Seven-something? And then you left, and..."*

Simpson: *"Yeah, I'm trying to think, did I leave? You know, I'm always ...I had to run and get my daughter some flowers. I was actually doing the recital, so I rushed and got her some flowers, and I came home, and then I called Paula as I was going to her house, and Paula wasn't home."*

Det. Vannatter: *Paula is your girlfriend?*

"Paula is your girlfriend" would not have been the follow up questioned I would have used. If you were the detective in this scenario, what would be a good follow up question(s) to O.J.'s answers?

Admission development

Once the investigator has obtained an admission, he/she has to develop it into a confession. The hardest point to determine in an interrogation is when a suspect is ready to confess. If the investigator moves too early, they may back the suspect into a denial. If they move to late, they may never reach that point again. This is a good time to kill their alibi.

"You stated earlier that you were at home watching television on the night of the incident. Is that correct?" "Yes, it is." "You also said that you ate pizza for dinner. Is that correct?" "Yes it is." First of all, a "home alone, watching television" scenario is not a very good alibi, but you'd never believe how often it is used. Here you can see the investigator is getting ready to kill the alibi. What part would you attack first? I'm almost positive that most of you would start out asking questions about the television: "What shows? At what time? What was the episode about?" are not bad questions, but, you're rather limited to the number of questions that you can ask. Let's take a look at the "pizza" instead and see how many questions I can come up with:

1. Did you make it yourself?
2. Was it store bought?
3. Was it delivered?
4. What type of pizza did you have? (Round or Square)
5. What time did you get it/have it delivered?
6. What topping(s) did you have?
7. How much did it cost?
8. What location did you buy it or have it delivered from?
9. Did you give the delivery person a tip?
10. Was the delivery person male/female?
11. What race was the delivery person?
12. Was the pizzeria busy when you were there?
13. How did you get to the pizzeria?
14. How many slices did you have?
15. What was the phone number you called?
16. What did the delivery person look like?

These are sixteen questions off the top of my head and you have to take into consideration any additional questions that may come from the answers they give. If you noticed one thing about my questions, what would it be? All of the answers can be verified! You may be able to think of even more, but you see there was a lot more versatility with the "pizza" then with the "television." You should also note that I wouldn't ask these questions in any particular order. This way you can easily trip them up if they are lying to you. Also, an alibi like this would be a good opportunity to use the "backwards to

forwards" technique of vetting an alibi. It requires the suspect
to tell his/her story backwards to the beginning. Anyone who
made up the story would not be able to do it.

When the investigator effectively "kills off" the alibi person
or story, they are ready to move beyond the admission and
into a confession or a detailed statement about who was
responsible for the incident in codefendant cases.

Documented on paper

Documenting the admission and/or confession on paper
is paramount. It is ideal to have the suspect write their own
confession out in their own hand writing. If the individual
cannot write, the police are allowed to write it for them and
he/she can OK it by signing their name to it. Taking the final
written statement encompasses the sequence of events that
took place during the interrogation. They will include the
bathroom breaks, meal and sleep breaks. Nothing can kill a
defense lawyer's argument about coercion than a statement
made by the suspect on how well they were treated! But the
most important reason to obtain a written, signed statement
is that it locks the suspect down. They become imprisoned by
their own words.

At the conclusion of the interrogation, the investigator
should present a lined, legal sized pad and pen to the
perpetrator and ask for their narrative or "explanation (not a
statement)" in writing. Even though the investigator is at the
end of the process, he/she should continue to avoid using
words that enlist "consequences" for suspect's actions. "Hi
John, please write down for me how you killed Mary and how
you dumped her body alongside of the road. This way the jury
doesn't have any qualms about sending you to the electric
chair," would not be a good way to start off. If necessary, the
investigator will sell the idea, "Don't you want to get your side
down on the record?" or "Don't you want to explain that it was
an accident and that it could have happened to anybody?"

The investigators should stay in the room during the
writing of the statement and if possible have an additional
witness in the room. The investigator should fight the urge to
write it for them when they are totally capable of doing so
themselves. When the suspect is done, review their statement
with them to make sure it is complete. Once the investigator

is satisfied with the results he/she will leave the room with the admission/confession and especially the pen! Investigators can never get sloppy and leave a potential weapon or escape device behind. The investigator must type a report detailing the events that transpired during the interrogation and the results, whether if they were able to obtain an admission or confession and a written statement. The term negative results are never used on any police reports. There is always something to report.

CI Tip Sheet

Make a number of copies of the original written statement and secure the original with the case folder.

Why in the world would a person confess and risk going to jail the rest of their lives? There is no guarantee that you are going to get the suspect to confess even after all of your hard work. The investigator has to understand that individuals want to get things off of their chest so they can feel better. Some religions offer Penance to confess their sins and move on with their lives and some people seek out the counsel of a psychologist to get their lives moving again by revealing what is bothering them. Some investigators are very easy to talk to especially when they have learned to effectively build rapport. It is human nature to want to talk through our problems.

There is an urban police legend that the "Guilty Always Sleep." When you have been hunting a perpetrator, especially after a long period of time, and you finally catch him/her and put them in the holding cell, something strange happens. Within a few minutes of putting them there, they curl up on the bench and go to sleep. This phenomenon, which I have personally experienced, could be explained rather easily. After being on the run, not sleeping well, nervous, paranoid, moving from place to place, constantly looking over their shoulder, the individual has no reason to do those things any longer and finally gets a chance to rest. The gig is up! Think for a moment on how you feel after you have taken a big exam or after a stressful week at work?

Reasons not to Confess

In the beginning of this chapter I listed all the reasons why people confess. Now, I'm going to cover why someone would not want to confess. There is a strong foundation to believe that people want to "confess" so they can move on. However, in criminal investigation the stakes are much higher. The consequences of coming clean could be a lengthy prison sentence, life behind bars or even the death penalty. Sometimes, people will not give a confession out of **FEAR**:

Financial repercussions
Embarrassment
Arrest and prosecution
Retaliation

Financial repercussions

The suspect knows that if he/she goes to jail there will be an immediate financial impact on their family. There is a huge expense if they hire their own attorney or if bail must be posted. Quite often the suspect's family has to mortgage their home or spend their entire life savings. Also, the victim or the victim's family may file a lawsuit in civil court seeking damages in a wrongful death or injury suit. No money equals: cannot pay bills or rent/mortgage, no clothes and no food on the table. etc. It is a major obstacle for investigators to overcome.

Embarrassment

Arrest and possible conviction for a crime can sever the social bonds between friends and family. Can they ever earn back the trust from family, friends and coworkers? The embarrassment affects the individual's self image; self esteem and may cause shock and rage from the public. No one I know would want their picture posted on the front page of the newspapers.

Arrest and prosecution

The thought of going to prison is deterrence enough for most people, especially those with little or no experience with the Criminal Justice System. Prison also puts an added expense and a burden on family members. Traveling expenses, lengthy commutes for visits all take a toll on the family. Eventually, they will stop coming. The worst thought about prison an individual can have is who or what awaits them in their cell.

Retaliation

Imagine the following scenario: Johnny Jones is a low-level drug dealer who gets into a dispute with the drug operations best earner. During the altercation, Johnny takes out his gun and shoots him in the head. What's the first thing that is going through Johnny's mind? "I'm a dead man." Most perpetrators have a fear that someone will take revenge against them or one of their family members and in some cases they are probably right. This is what happens in cases that involve dealing in illegal narcotics or organized crime. Live by the sword, die by the sword.

In conclusion, the student should by now have an understanding why interrogation is often called an art form. An investigator just isn't born with the skill of interrogation; it is a skill which is developed through experience and education. The student is encouraged to develop skills through their interactions with others and to seek out reference materials about the subject. There are many excellent books on the subject and I encourage you to explore several as you begin to develop your interview and interrogation techniques.

Here is a chart that lists the differences between Interview and Interrogation:

Interview	Interrogation
No legal requirements	Legal requirements - Miranda
Little or moderate planning before	Extensive planning and studying
Investigator does most of the listening	Investigator does most of the talking

Interview	Interrogation
Private or semi private location	Total privacy
Cooperation is likely	Cooperation unlikely
Calm and pleasant	Hostile and adversarial
Seeking information	Testing that information
Victim/witness	Suspect/perpetrator
Not suspected of any wrongdoing	Suspected of wrongdoing

Questions for Discussion and Review:

1.   Johnny Jones asks for a lawyer while in custody and all questioning stopped. An hour later he changes his mind and calls the investigator back into the room and makes a full written and oral confession. Will this confession hold up in court? Why or why not?

2.   What is rapport building?

3.   What is the most important reason to obtain a signed, written statement from the suspect?

4.   Do the police always have to read Miranda to persons in custody?

5.   Why is it difficult to tell a story backwards if you haven't told the truth?

6.   What are the types of questions that should never be used by investigators?

7.   Why does giving someone a way out of a problem work?

8.   What are some of the reasons why people will not confess?

9.   What are some of the reasons why people confess?

10.   What are the instances where a suspect has an absolute right to counsel?

11.   Why is it important for an investigator to have the "knowledge of how and why" of the case before they start an interrogation?

12.   What is the reason for documenting the treatment of a suspect in custodial interrogation?

13.   What is wrong with asking a leading question?

14. Why should investigators strive to keep witnesses/ victims separated?

15. Who should conduct the interview and why?

16. In addition to the examples given, what are other techniques can be used to build rapport?

17. Why do you think that opened ended questions are best to use first in an interview?

Chapter 8

Introduction to Special Investigations

"No, I've never thought about divorce in all these 35 years of marriage, but I did think of murder a few times."
— Ruth Graham

Every law enforcement agency in the United States (totaling over 19,000) must report the eight major felonies to the FBI, with a few exceptions. For example, New York City does not track the crime of Arson for statistical purposes. Each year the FBI gathers these figures and publishes, Crime in the United States, which is formally known to law enforcement and Criminal Justice students as the Uniform Crime Report, or the UCR for short. Anytime you hear that "crime is up" or "crime is down," these are the crimes that the media and the politicians are referring to. The eight major felonies are broken up into two (2) main categories: Crimes Against the Person and Crimes Against Property.

This chapter begins the "meat and potatoes" of criminal investigation. These are the crimes that investigators will spend most of their time investigating. However as you will see, there are many subdivisions of the major felonies. These crimes are equally heinous as the eight majors, but are not required to be reported for statistical purposes. But these crimes hold valuable importance to law enforcement.

Note: The terms: 8 Majors, 8 Major Felonies, Index Crimes all mean the same thing.

Every good investigator seeks justice for those that can no longer do it for themselves or who are unable to do it. A closed case, especially a murder, begins the healing process for the victim's family and friends by providing closure.

I would like to introduce you to **MR Rob F. BuGGA**, the eight major felonies in order of severity (from worst to bad):

1. **M**urder
2. **R**ape

3. **Rob**bery

4. **F**elony Assault

5. **Bu**rglary
6. **G**rand Larceny
7. **G**rand larceny Auto
8. **A**rson

Murder, Rape, Robbery and Felony Assault are known as the Crimes Against the Person. These four (4) crimes are considered the most violent, recognizable and most reported of all the offenses. This is not to say that other crimes are not as important as these, but they are the crimes often perpetrated on society by people. Not every one of the 8 Majors has an "Attempted" charge if the perpetrator is not successful. For example, you intend to kill your friend and shoot them, but they do not die. That case will be carried as a Felony Assault and not an Attempted Murder. The perpetrator dropped down in prosecution purposes on the scale from #1 to #4. Try to explain that rationale to the victim.

Burglary, Grand Larceny, Grand Larceny Auto and Arson are known as the Crimes Against Property. This grouping of the 8 Majors tells us that the worst thing you can do is enter someone's home and take their property.

CI Tip Sheet

Investigators have to know the CAPs:

Crimes Against the Person –
     Murder, Rape, Robbery and Felony Assault
Crimes Against Property –
     Burglary, Grand Larceny, GLA and Arson

A quality preliminary investigation by the first officer(s) on the scene is the key to solving any crime. A properly secured scene coupled with the proper notifications will start the investigation off on the right foot. Due to the violent nature in these crimes, the investigator should rely on Locard's Exchange Principle (for more see the Crime Scene Protocol) and special attention must be given to physical evidence. I'm sure you can imagine the amount of criminal incidents that occur on any given day in a large metropolitan area. This is another reason why the 8 Major Felonies have been chosen.

The 8 Major felonies, as well as other investigations, can be disposed of for classification purposes in the following four (4) **REAL** ways:

Remain Open
Exceptional Clearance
Arrest
Leads exhausted

Remain Open

Depending on the investigation, the case can always remain open. Homicides, rapes and crimes belonging to a pattern will remain open pending further investigation. Murder cases are never closed until an arrest is made. When a case is left open, it is always in the back of the investigator's mind that someday they will get that lucky break, develop new investigative leads, changes in relationships between people and the discovery of new DNA technologies. A break can come in the form of an arrest where the perpetrator wants to make a deal with a prosecutor to provide information about an open investigation or from the person who is on their death bed and makes a dying declaration.

Exceptional Clearance

Exceptional clearance, an EC for short, occurs when the police have probable cause to make an arrest, but cannot do so because of an unusual circumstance beyond their control. An unusual circumstance is one where the perpetrator is dead or in a jurisdiction that does not have a treaty with the United States that allows extraditing the perpetrator for prosecution, i.e., Cuba. There are several unfriendly governments who refuse to extradite their citizens to the United States. The investigator will close the case as an EC and file the appropriate "flags" that will trip if the individual attempts to enter the United States.

Arrest

An arrest occurs when the police have established sufficient probable cause (See the Criminal Investigative Process). The police take the individual into custody so they can answer for the crime that they have been charged with in front of a court of law.

Leads exhausted

A case is also closed when the investigator runs out of viable leads or has encountered a fatal blow to the investigation. A fatal blow can come from a variety of things, but the most common are: when the victim cannot pick out the perpetrator in an array or lineup (See Eyewitness Identification Procedures), the loss or destruction of evidence or the lack of cooperation from the victim. Sometimes a victim cannot spend the time necessary to help the police because of family and work obligations or some victims have bad intentions and would rather "take care of it themselves." An investigator cannot force a victim to help.

Questions for Discussion and Review:

1. What are the circumstances when a case can be closed as an Exceptional Clearance?

2. If someone is shot and they don't die, what crime would the perpetrator be charged with?

Chapter 9

Crimes Against the Person

Murder

"Murder, though it has no tongue, will speak with most miraculous organ."

— Hamlet, Act II Scene II

Murder is as the most heinous crime that one individual can perpetrate on another. Murder is defined by the UCR as the willful killing of one human being by another. Simply put, you intend the death of someone and you cause death. The number one circumstance surrounding an act of homicide is that the parties involved had some sort of argument that precipitated the event. I'm sure that if we were able to know the circumstances behind each argument, the most prevalent reasons behind the crime would be love, money and drugs. These three make up what I call the Homicide Triangle (Figure 9.1). Love should be at the top of the triangle because it brings out the strongest emotions. Investigators should use the Homicide Triangle when developing motives for a murder. When people in relationships are trapped within the Triangle, eventually someone is going to get hurt or killed.

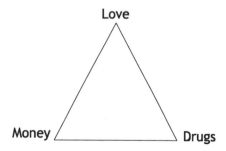

Figure 9.1

There is a strange twist on how attempted murder is counted in the UCR. If someone intends to kill someone, but fails to do so, they would be charged with felony assault, the number 4 crime on the scale of the 8 Major Crimes.

A perpetrator does not anticipate the wheels they set in motion when they choose murder as the answer to solve their problem(s). Investigators take all crimes committed against innocent people seriously, but the crimes of murder and rape seem to bring out the best in investigators. An interesting dynamic takes place during a homicide investigation. Investigators that never seem to get along or talk to one another, work together and investigators that usually do the bare minimum suddenly are Sherlock Holmes. If you speak to any investigator retired or active, they can all tell you about one particular case that couldn't be solved and how it still haunts them.

Take a moment and reflect on the concept of Cold Case Homicide Squads. Police departments, with limited budgets, spend a ton of money on cases that haven't been solved, sometimes for decades. The federal government has also recognized the importance of Cold Case Squads and provides millions of dollars in grant money for departments to keep these cases active.

A cold case squad's function is twofold:

(1) Protect the public from future occurrences and
(2) Provide closure for the victim's family members and friends.

In the context of criminal investigation, murder is the most fascinating, intriguing and awe inspiring of all for investigators, researchers and students. The act of taking someone's life for no apparent reason is incomprehensible to the average person. There are many questions raised during a murder investigation: *Why was this person chosen? Who was responsible? How did they do it?* and *Why did they do it?* to name a few.

Murder is the exemplar of criminal investigations. The techniques and strategies used to solve the ultimate crime against humanity can be used to solve all of the others. An investigator must know **TIM** in order to successfully develop suspects during a murder investigation:

Time of Death
Identity of the Victim
Manner of Death

Time of Death

One of the most important determinations in a death investigation is what time did the person die? Also know as the Postmortem Interval (PMI), the time of death aids the investigator in a suspicious death/murder in establishing the following: it can prove or disprove a suspect's alibi, provide a starting point for the investigative timeline and provide a marker for the 24 – 48 hours prior to individual's death to establish a victimology. Unfortunately, estimating time of death is controlled by factors out of the investigator's hands. Like the old song by Chicago, "Does anyone really know what time it is?" Unless you were with the person when they died and they were hooked up to an EKG monitor, no one will really know for sure.

It is called estimating time of death (ETD) for a reason. ETD is affected by so many factors that have nothing to do with the incident which caused the person to die. For example, was the body inside or outside? Did it happen during the cold or warm months? Was the person sick? Fever? Was the person engaged in some sort of physical activity prior to death? How much or how little clothes did they have on? How much did they weigh? etc. I think you get the picture. This is why it is called "estimating" or "approximating" time of death. It is not an exact science. The investigator should never take these changes in the body as the final decision, but only as a guide in establishing the ETD.

CI Tip Sheet

An investigator must **CHEW** on these factors that affect the time of death:

Clothing worn
How much did they weigh
Environmental temperature and conditions
Where the body was found

Any questions that the investigator has regarding changes in the body should be directed to the responding forensic pathologist.

You might ask if it is not an exact science, why bother wasting time trying to figure out the time of death? As you previously learned, the investigator needs to fulfill three (3) elements in order to have a suspect. These elements are known as **MOM**: The **M**eans, **O**pportunity and the **M**otive. Estimating time of death has all to do with establishing the *Opportunity* to commit the crime and either prove or disprove an alibi. Remember, if the investigator cannot fulfill all of the elements of **MOM**, they do not have a perpetrator! No matter how bad they "like" this person for the crime, the investigator must keep digging for witnesses and physical evidence, preferably, physical evidence.

The confusion about the ETD often begins with a pronunciation of death by Emergency Medical Service (EMS) workers or even doctors. The time of death is often recorded by a doctor or EMS when they walk in the door, see a person who is obviously dead, checks their watch and say, "he/she is dead." The time on a death certificate is often indicated as "date and time of death" or "date and time found dead" (Dr. Monica Smiddy, MD, e-mail conversation, February 17, 2009). This information is only for reporting or statistical purposes and should not be used as the "real" time of death. The investigator has to use the facts of the case and drill down to a more exact time frame.

To help the investigator estimate the time of death, the following changes in the body should be used as a template to aid in arriving to the closest possible time. Remember, the following information and facts happen under the perfect conditions. These are the changes in the body that many investigators use to estimating time of death. There are other indicators, such as insect activity (entomology) and stomach contents, but for the everyday investigator or student, these are the changes in the body that you should concentrate on.

In many homicide investigations there is a delay from the time the incident happens until the body is discovered. The body may not be discovered for minutes, hours, days, weeks or longer and in some cases, never. The precious time lost is only one of the many obstacles that an investigator will have to overcome. For this reason, investigators must maintain

A SHARP Eye when it comes to changes in the body post-mortem so an estimated time of death can be established. In addition, the interviews with the first officers on the scene are extremely important in death cases. The question, "What was the temperature (hot/cold) in the room when you entered?" must be added to your list of prospective questions.

Adipocere

Scene Markers
Hypostasis (Livor Mortis or Lividity)
Algor Mortis
Rigor Mortis
Putrefaction

Eye Fluid (Vitreous Humor)

Adipocere

Adipocere, also known as grave wax, is a grayish white or tan waxy-like substance that forms on the body due to the breakdown of fat during putrefaction (decomposition). It commonly occurs on bodies that are found in cool places or in water anytime between two (2) weeks to one month. Adipocere has also been discovered on bodies that have been buried (in or not in a casket) for a while. Adipocere is affected by temperature and insects (Australian Museum, 2003).

Scene Markers

Scene markers are items that an investigator may find at the location that may aid them in determining an approximate time of death. The last newspaper, the date stamp on un-opened/opened letters or bills, television program guide opened to a specific page, credit card/ATM or cash register receipts, expiration dates on dairy products or food, DVD rentals, prescription bottles, etc. This type of information can be matched up with facts gathered during the investigative canvass, or from friends and/or family members.

CI Tip Sheet

Scene markers can be a **PRIME** source of information used in estimating the time of death:

Papers
Receipts
Interviews
Mail
Expiration dates on food products

Hypostasis (Livor Mortis or Lividity)

When the heart stops pumping were does the blood go? The law of gravity takes over and draws the blood from the arteries into the smaller capillaries. The blood causes a purplish/reddish color in the dependent areas of the body. Parts of the body that are in contact with a surface will appear white or "blanched." This is caused by the compression of the smaller blood vessels. For example, an individual dies on their back and is not found until fifteen (15) hours later. The investigator should expect to see the purplish/reddish color of the skin except the upper back, heels of the feet, buttocks and back of the head. This is an important investigative tool for the investigator to identify if the body has been moved prior to their arrival.

Hypostasis begins immediately upon death and becomes evident within 30 minutes. Lividity tends to reach maximum coloration in about eight (8) to twelve (12) hours, when it becomes "fixed" (DiMaio & DiMaio, 2001, p. 23). If the body is moved after lividity has become "fixed" the coloration will not disappear.

You can conduct a test on yourself. Take your index finger and press it against your thumb until it turns a bright red and let it go. For a split second you can see the white or blanched impression of your thumb on your index finger. This is the reason why lividity can never be mistaken for bruising.

CI Tip Sheet

Here is any easy way to remember what changes in the body occur after death, which are related to hypostasis (lividity): Hypostasis is really spelled with three (3) **Ps**

    Pooling of blood in the dependent areas of the body
    Purplish in color
    Permanent or fixed in eight (8) to twelve (12) hours

Algor Mortis

Algor Mortis is the cooling of the body after death. Our "normal" core body temperature is 98.6°. After death, our body will lose approximately 1.5° every hour until it reaches the ambient, or surrounding, temperature of the room. The body temperature is taken using a thermometer called a liver stick, which is sometimes not used in the liver. The investigator will count backwards to obtain an estimated time of death. For example, the pathologist obtains a body temperature reading of 95.6°. Easy math would indicate a change of 3° or 3°/1.5° or the person has been dead approximately two (2) hours. Because of the myriad of factors that can affect one's temperature, Algor Mortis is often considered unreliable.

CI Tip Sheet

When you think of Algor Mortis think of **AM**: Time

Rigor Mortis

Rigor Mortis, Latin for "stiffening of the joints," starts within one (1) to three (3) hours after death. Rigor Mortis sets in the body all at the same time, but it is most noticeable in the jaw first. Rigor Mortis is caused by the buildup of lactic acid in the joints causing them to "freeze" temporarily. It takes approximately ten (10) to fifteen (15) hours for the body to reach full Rigor and then will disappear within thirty-six (36) hours. Think of Rigor Mortis in the terms of a Bell Curve at the peak would be full rigor. Of course, other factors will greatly affect the onset of Rigor Mortis, such as the heat (excels) and the cold (slows).

Rigor Mortis is an excellent way to determine if a body has been moved. It will be quite apparent to the investigator when a body in the stages of rigor has been moved. If an investigator walks into the crime scene and sees the victim lying on his back and his arms are perpendicular to the ground, they know the body was moved. Only in cartoons does this happen. A question about who moved the body and why should be added to your list to ask upon your arrival at the scene, "Did you touch the body?" followed by, "Why did you touch the body if rigor mortis was present?"

Putrefaction (Decomposition)

The last stage of death is known as Putrefaction or Decomposition. As Rigor Mortis passes, the skin in the stomach area will begin to turn green. This is due to the buildup of methane gas from bacteria and enzymes in the stomach and intestines. The general time from for Putrefaction to begin is as follows:

- One (1) week in the air
- Two (2) weeks in the water
- Eight (8) weeks in the soil

CI Tip Sheet

An easy way to remember when decomposition starts is Paul Revere's famous quote, "One if by land, and two if by sea."

Eye Fluid (Vitreous Humor)

The vitreous humor is the clear liquid found in between the lens and the retina of the eyeball. After death levels of potassium increase which causes the cornea to become cloudy. Vitreous humor is extracted at autopsy so the level of potassium in the fluid can be determined.

An investigator can use the above time frames to help estimate the time of death. Once again, the investigator must be mindful of anything that can change the rate of decomposition by speeding it up or slowing it down. Algor, rigor, and livor mortis, decomposition and scene markers can all support the investigation community in estimating the time of death. The investigator must remain objective and constantly be aware of the factors that are out of his/her control, i.e., environment, clothing, etc.

Identity of the Victim

The initial investigative step in a homicide case is to identify the victim. This is not as easy as it sounds. Yes, you can reach into the guy's back pocket and see if he has a wallet, but it's not always that easy. Even if they possessed a driver's license, a dead body will be listed as unidentified until a next of kin is notified and can make a positive identification. An investigator will use a license or other form of identification as only "tentative identification." To jump start the investigation, it is a common practice to take a picture of the decedent's face to show a friend or family member to obtain a tentative ID. This alone is not a positive identification. In order to avoid misidentification, a family member must then ID the body at the morgue not only to the forensic pathologist but to the case investigator as well.

If an investigator has to wait for fingerprints or DNA examinations to come back, the investigation will be delayed even longer. The longer it takes to identify the victim, the further away your perpetrator gets. If no tentative identification is available or the fingerprints are not in the system, the investigator will conduct a search of known missing person cases and attempt to match one up to the victim.

Why is the identity of the victim so important to the investigator? When we know who the victim is we know: where he lived, who his family was, where he worked, who his friends and relatives were, who his enemies were and who would benefit the most from his death. According to the UCR, most people are murdered by someone they know, especially when the victim is a spouse. The identity of the victim provides the framework to launch the investigation.

There are two (2) tracks a murder investigation will take:

(1) When we know who the perpetrator is and only have to locate them and
(2) When the perpetrator is unknown or UNSUB (unknown subject).

Both tracks require a "hunt" for the perpetrator with varying degrees of investigative techniques. Of course, it is easier to track down people we know based on previous contacts, places and things that were discussed in the "Follow up Investigation."

"Why did someone want this person dead?" is always a good place to start. When you concentrate on the "why or reasons" (motive), it can sometimes lead you to the "who." Take this scenario for example: An executive from the carting industry is gunned down in his driveway. What are some of the motives that pop into your head prior to your arrival at the crime scene? First, most would create the following formula in your mind: carting industry + gunned down in driveway = Mob Hit. I know I would. Other motives that should be explored in your mind about this scenario are: a possible love triangle, insurance money, revenge, a subordinate who is next in line (greed and ambition), and unpaid debts. Hypothesis formulation isn't rocket science when it comes to crime. The previous scenario doesn't sound like a random act, but a coordinated, planned murder based on information provided to the perpetrator, i.e., what time they left for work, where they would be at a particular time, etc.

Where would you start this investigation? Your first hypothesis (mob hit) would be based on background information obtained during a victimology (see Follow Up Investigation). Does the victim have known ties to organized crime (OC)? If so, where are they in the "food chain? Were they a soldier or a boss?" If this information is either unknown or unavailable, the investigator will look into the people closest to the victim, starting with the wife. But would the investigator go straight to the wife? No. They would get to the wife in time through a circuitous path. A smart investigator would only interview the wife after speaking to friends, coworkers and family of both the victim and the wife. This information can help an investigator validate or invalidate what the wife will tell them.

For instance, a family friend tells the investigator that, "the two of them fought like cats and dogs and that he thinks the husband had a girlfriend." As an investigator wouldn't you want to know this before interviewing the wife? How else would you know if she was lying to you? What if the investigator didn't seek out information from others and went to the wife first? She could stall the investigation enough to disappear. As an investigator, I never asked a question to *a suspect* that I didn't already know the answer.

Manner of Death

Death investigations cover what is known to a forensic pathologist as the manner of death. A forensic pathologist is someone that applies the principles and knowledge of the medical sciences to problems in the field of law. Under the title "Manner of Death" on a death certificate, the forensic pathologist will list one of the (5) five manners of death listed and explained below. The manner of death is not to be confused with the cause of death. They are two different things. The cause of death is an injury or disease that produces death. Cause of death examples can range from heart disease to a gunshot wound.

A forensic pathologist attends **NASH U** when determining the manner of death:

Natural
Accidental
Suicide
Homicide**

Undetermined

** The term homicide is used only for definitional purposes—there is no criminal charge of "Homicide," it would be Murder. I am positive that police departments wouldn't want to have a unit called the "Murder Squad."

An investigator will respond to every dead person, no matter what the manner of death is. Why? Crime scenes can be staged to appear to be something else and the only way to determine what happened is with a careful inspection of the scene. Every death will be deemed suspicious until the investigation is complete and a conferral is made with the pathologist. Even in obvious natural deaths, investigators will take photos and conduct a cursory investigation by inter- viewing family, friends and doctors. Investigators will contact the doctor directly and determine if the person was under their direct care and if they are willing to sign off on the death certificate. When the doctor will sign the death certificate, the body will be released to the custody of the family.

Natural and Accidental deaths are self explanatory and I am not going to spend a lot of time on them. Natural deaths include long battles with illness such as cancer or from old age. Accidental deaths can occur from car crashes or falling off the roof of the house while making repairs. These occur- rences are not crimes and once the determination is made and foul play has been ruled out, the investigation will be closed as accidents/naturals and no further investigation will occur.

Suicide

Suicide is defined as taking one's own life. The latest figures from the Center of Disease Control and Prevention (CDC) show that there were 32,439 suicides in the United States in 2004. Suicide is the eleventh leading cause of death in the United States, compared to murder which is the 15th (15,241). An investigator has more than twice the chance of investigating a suicide as they do a murder. Firearms are the preferred method of choice amongst males (57.6%) and poisoning is the most preferred method for females (39.1%).

The goal of an investigator at the scene of a suicide is to determine if it is in fact a suicide and not a homicide. He/she will accomplish this task by a careful examination of evidence at the scene and speaking with family and friends. A check of police records can determine if the person was ever brought to a hospital for a past attempt at suicide or had received medical attention for psychological issues. As noted earlier, men choose more violent methods of committing suicide then women and are more successful at it. Based on the statistics, an investigator can expect to find a weapon at the scene of a male suicide and sleeping pills if it is a woman.

In my experience with suicide investigations, it is very rare to find a suicide note, so the investigator cannot rely on any leads to identify the causes of the suicide right away. In a

2006 study conducted in Japan on suicide, only 32.5% of people left suicide notes (Japan Times Online, June 8, 2007) and a smaller study in Florida by Dr. Richard Hall (n.d.), found that only 10% of people left a suicide note. With those kinds of statistics, investigators should be leery when they encounter a suicide note. If a note is encountered, investigators can enlist the help of a forensic linguistics expert who may determine if the note is authentic. No one should handle the note unless they have gloves on. The document should be secured in a plastic security type envelope and sent to the laboratory. The investigator should write on the security envelope *before* they place the note inside of it.

Some killers will attempt to throw off the investigation by staging a homicide to appear as if it were a suicide. It is not far from the realm of reality that a perpetrator at one time took a criminal investigation course, read a book or watched crime shows on television all in the hopes of making themselves a better criminal. Clues of a staging can range from a bullet to the left temple, when the person was right handed, a gunshot wound to the back of the head, a gunshot wound but a gun was not recovered at the scene, a gunshot wound with a firearm at the scene but no gunshot residue (GSR) on the victim's hand or a sign of a struggle (knocked over furniture, broken glass), or the presence of defensive wounds, or the nature and extent of the injuries sustained. An investigator develops additional information about the person from canvasses. Did anyone hear arguing, multiple gunshots, a dog barking or know about previous suicide attempts or past domestic/financial/gambling problems?

Bad guys aren't the only ones to stage scenes, especially when dealing with a suicide investigation. There have been times when family members have staged a suicide to look like a homicide. You might ask, "Why would someone what to do that?" Sometimes it is a cultural embarrassment for the family and sometimes it has to do with life insurance money. Insurance companies will not pay out on a policy when the person took their own life.

The most important interviews are conducted with friends and family members. The investigator conducts a victimology (see Follow Up Investigation) on the person. In a suicide case, the victimology is commonly referred to as a psychological autopsy. A psychological autopsy can provide an insight into the deceased person's mind and what was going on, good or bad, in their life. Financial problems, health problems, depression and relationship problems are common causes for an individual to take their own life.

Homicide

As discussed earlier, the term "homicide" is strictly for definitional purposes and never is used in lieu of "murder" as a charge. In a homicide investigation an investigator must fight tunnel vision and the urge to go directly to the victim's body. That is easier said then done; it is human nature to be drawn to it. The only thing that can prevent the inadvertent destruction of evidence is a slow, methodical search of the crime scene that surrounds the body. Remember, the location where the body is found is the primary crime scene because that is where most of the evidence will be found.

Homicide victims should have their hands "bagged" in paper by the crime scene technicians in case the victim scratched their attacker. The scrapings for skin cells will be conducted at autopsy by the forensic pathologist and not by the crime scene technician.

Undetermined

The category undetermined is also known as a C.U.P.P.I. (pronounced cup-e): Cause Undetermined Pending Police Investigation. When the medical examiner cannot determine the manner of death, they will send the case back to the investigator as a C.U.P.P.I. with a series of questions that they would like answered out. This is why it is extremely important for the investigator to attend the autopsy. He/she maybe able to answer questions or provide the evidence the medical examiner needs to make the determination on the proper manner of death classification.

There is a time limit on a C.U.P.P.I. case in some jurisdictions. If the case remains undetermined for a period of time, generally within a year, it will turn into a homicide statistic. This is not the ideal situation for any investigation, especially a homicide investigation. The longer the investigation goes, the less likely it will be solved.

The crime of Murder has a little brother, his name is Manslaughter. Manslaughter occurs when an individual intends to cause a serious physical injury, but kills the person. For instance, in a fit of rage a wife picks up a frying pan and throws it at her husband, striking him in the head, killing him. Her intent was to hurt him, not to kill him. Unfortunately for him, she had good aim and he had terrible luck.

The Autopsy Protocol

An autopsy is process by which a forensic pathologist, medical examiner, coroner determines the manner and cause of death. It involves the complete exterior and interior examination of a dead human body including a full set of X-rays, determining the angle of trajectory in shooting cases and the type of knife used in a stabbing. The following exemplars will be taken from the victim at the autopsy: fingernail clippings, hair & blood samples.

There is a difference between the medical examiner and a coroner. A medical examiner is a medical doctor and coroners are not. A medical examiner is an appointed position and a coroner is an elected position who use medical personnel to assist in determining the manner of death. According to the Center for Disease Control (CDC) in 2004, 21 states and the District of Columbia have a medical examiner system, 10 states have coroner-based systems and 19 states have both systems (Nolte, Hanzlick, Payne, Kroger, Oliver, Baker, McGowan, DeJong, Bell, Guarner, Shieh, Zaki).

The investigator must view an autopsy as an extension of a crime scene because it may provide additional information and/or evidence. How else would an investigator gain possession of bullets removed from the body? An investigator must make an **APP**ointment to see the forensic pathologist/medical examiner/coroner the very next day. Yes, even on weekends and holidays! Death never takes a day off.

Attendance
Paperwork
Participate

Attendance

An investigator *must appear* at every autopsy that involves a homicide, suicide or suspicious death and be prepared to answer any questions that the pathologist may have. If the lead investigator cannot appear do to the investigation, i.e., conducting live lineups or processing the arrest, another investigator who was physically at the scene and is current with the investigation will go in their place.

Paperwork

The investigator should take the case folder, crime scene photos, a copy of the evidence log, any sketches made of the scene or any other reports that may be necessary to the autopsy. If the pathologist is looking for information to validate their examination results, these items may provide the evidence to make a determination on manner and cause of death. These documents can help make the decision to label the manner of death something other than a C.U.P.P.I.

Participate

An investigator is not solely an observer at an autopsy. They should participate by asking questions and taking notes. The investigator should capture the following information for the investigative report: manner and cause of death, depth and general nature of wounds and other contributing factors that were identified through the autopsy.

Questions for Discussion and Review:

1. What is the difference between cause of death and manner of death?

2. Why is the manner of death important to know?

3. In addition to the examples already given, list some other causes of death.

4. Why was the term homicide used to define the act of murder?

5. What could be a reason for a jurisdiction not to report one of the eight major crimes?

6. Should assisted suicide continued to be treated as a crime? Explain.

7. What are some of the factors that affect estimating time of death? How do they affect it?

8. The police develop probable cause to arrest an individual for murder on an old case but discover that the perpetrator is now in federal lockup for life. What case closing disposition would be used?

9. Why could a murder investigation be used as an exemplar to investigate other crimes?

10. An investigator submits fingerprints of an unknown victim. The prints come back to a match and a notification that the victim is wanted for murder. What does an investigator do about the other opened case?

11. Why is the location where the body is found become the primary crime scene?

Rape

"Rape is the only crime in which the victim becomes the accused."

— Criminologist Fred Adler

According to the FBI's Uniform Crime Report (FBI, 2009), Rape is defined as the carnal knowledge of a female forcibly and against her will. Any attempts via force or threats of force are considered rape. Any attempt at a rape will be classified as if it happened. In simple terms, rape is when someone has sexual intercourse, penis to vagina, with another person against their will by force or by a lack of consent. You will see in a few moments that state governments have defined other ways that the crime of rape can be charged in addition to forcible compulsion.

The crime of rape is not considered the most heinous crime (number 2) one human can do to another, but some, including myself would argue. When someone is murdered, the pain and suffering lives on with the family and not the victim. Often rape is a crime that leaves the victim violated, their life and relationships in ruin and sometimes emotionally distraught. Sometimes the victim takes their own life because of it. Rape is a crime that often leaves the victim blaming herself and sometimes leaves the public to blame the victim too. *"If she was home at a decent time, this would never have happened, if she wasn't wearing those clothes..."* and the list goes on.

Rape has long been one of the most under reported crimes throughout the United States. Several factors may exist on why this is so: The victim may believe the police won't catch the perpetrator, they may be worried about unsympathetic treatment by the Criminal Justice System, embarrassment, fear of being attacked again or the fact that 66% of all reported rapes the victim knew who her attacker was. To help with the decision to report the crime and preserve evidence, the U.S. Government has made it mandatory for states to conduct, "Jane Doe Rape Kits," which are kept on file in case the victim changes her mind at a later date and wishes to go forward with the investigation (Wyatt, 2008).

The 2009 UCR reported the following statistics for the crime of rape:

- More than 88,097 of reported rapes were committed by some sort of force
- A forcible rape occurs every 5.8 minutes in the United States
- 66% of all rapes that were reported, the victim knew her attacker
- 41% of all rapes were closed by arrest

Different jurisdictions throughout the United States have gone beyond the "forcibly against her will" and have added other ways that a perpetrator can be charged with this crime. The investigator should be familiar with the acronym, **FLIP**, so they can remember the factors for the crime of rape:

The highest category of rape involves the following elements:

Forcible compulsion
Lack of consent because of the victim's age
Incapacitated mentally or mentally disabled
Physically helpless

Forcible compulsion

The highest degree rape charge occurs when the perpetrator uses any force, threatened or implied. It could be done with or without a weapon or through the use of physical force. The threats do not even have to be against the victim, they could be made to a child or some other person. "If you don't cooperate, I am going to burn your house down." Forcible rape would bring a higher class of felony in most, if not all, jurisdictions.

Lack of consent because of the victim's age

State and local governments have set different age limits for when a person, generally the male, can engage in sexual activity with a female. For some of the age categories, statutory rape charges would apply, which are not counted in the FBI's UCR report. For instance, in New York State if he/she is 21 years of age or more and engages in sexual intercourse with another person that is 16, they would be charged with Rape 3°, a statutory rape. This rape would not be included in the numbers reported to the FBI for statistical purposes.

Incapacitated mentally or mentally disabled

Consent cannot be given by a person who is incapacitated mentally or mentally disabled. The difference between the two categories are: if someone puts something in a drink (date rape drug) which renders them incapacitated and has sex with them, they would be charged with rape. A person, who is mentally disabled or has a mental defect, cannot give consent. Therefore, a person who has sex with a mentally disabled person will also be charged with rape.

Physically helpless

The victim in this category is unconscious or for some other reason cannot communicate their lack of consent.

The Rape Investigation

There are always two (2) crime scenes in rape cases:

(1) The location where it happened, if it were inside or outside would be cordoned off and secured like any other crime scene, and
(2) the victim themselves.

The investigator would treat the victim as the primary crime scene because they are the best chance of obtaining physical evidence. Because rape is such a violent offense, the likelihood of locating transfer evidence such as: hair, fibers, fingernail scrapings (Locard's Exchange Principle) is good as well as finding body fluids such as: blood, semen, and saliva on bite mark evidence. Bite mark evidence is often found in rapes because of the vicious behavior exhibited by the perpetrator during the event. It is evidence that cannot be overlooked.

Saliva is a great source of DNA evidence and must be secured properly by using swabs. A swab is a wooden stick with a ball of cotton on the end of it. The location where the victim was bit will be swabbed in a two step process. The technique is the wet/dry method. The first swab is dipped in distilled water (water that has had all impurities removed) and the area will be swabbed, then the dry swab will be used over the same location. The swabs are then inserted in a cardboard container and submitted to the laboratory for examination.

CI Tip Sheet

Two Crime Scenes in rape cases:

    (1) The location where it happened
    (2) The victim themselves

An ambulance will be requested to the scene to transport the victim to the hospital for further investigation. The investigator must go with the victim because they are a crime scene! The first and most difficult task for the investigator is to ask the victim if they have showered, gone to the bathroom or cleaned themselves up in anyway. Cleaning and urinating can wash away DNA evidence as well as any drugs that may have been given to the victim.

Sex crime cases are extremely difficult to investigate because of the sensitive nature of the topic and the traumatic effects it has on the victim. The investigator must ask the tough questions though. It may not be pleasant, but their initial approach, their sincerity and empathy are important factors in easing the pain of the victim. A series of photographs must be taken of any bruises, bite marks or physical evidence found on the victim's body as well as the scene. Photos will be taken without a ruler and then with a ruler, especially evidence of bite marks.

Once at the hospital, a doctor will give the victim an examination and determine if they require immediate medical attention. There is no reason for the investigator to be in the room during the examination. Investigators must provide privacy and avoid causing additional embarrassment to the victim by being present in the room.

Depending on the preliminary investigation, the doctor will prepare a sexual offense evidence kit and/or a drug facilitated sexual offense evidence kit. Both kits are designed to collect and preserve evidence for prosecution, including the victim's clothing. The sex offense evidence kit contains slides, swabs and containers to collect evidence. The drug facilitated kit requires a blood sample for toxicology testing. Date rape drugs such as Ecstasy, Rohyponol and GHB are fast acting depressants that target the central nervous system, often incapacitating the victim both physically and mentally (Office for Victims of Crime, 2008, p. 44). After the doctor completes the exam and the kit(s), he/she will seal the kit and sign their name on the front of the kit, starting the chain of custody. When the investigator receives the kit, he/she will sign underneath the doctor's signature. The kit will then be delivered to the laboratory for testing.

Investigators will put together a complete victimology on the victim (see Chapter 5). Information from the background checks may shed some light on who the perpetrator is. After the examinations are completed the investigator must sit down with the victim and chronicle the timeline of events, before, during and after the incident. Where did she meet him? What did he say during the event? The police will not wait for the DNA testing to come back before launching the investigation. Does the victim know the perpetrator? If not, the investigator will ask the victim to view police photo books. If the victim cannot identify anyone through photos a police sketch artist should be called in.

The location of the rape will be treated just like any other crime scene, but special attention will be given to the room where the act occurred, generally the bedroom. The investigator will ensure that the bed sheets and any clothing that was worn are secured and packaged in paper. Remember, all evidence that can contain body fluids will *always* be secured in paper and *never* in plastic. The crime scene tech will make an intensive search for hair follicles and other trace evidence. However, the investigator may have some Fourth Amendment issues to be concerned with. For instance, if the crime happened inside of a location where the suspect has an expectation of privacy, then the police will need to obtain a search warrant. If you consider the fact that most victims of rape know their attackers, there is a good possibility that they live together. Also, if investigators develop probable cause that the suspect has stored, has the ingredients for or has made a date rape drug, then a warrant must be obtained.

The bathroom can be a treasure trove of forensic evidence. When we are soiled where do we go? The perpetrator often uses the bathroom to wash after the event. Many times the perpetrator will remove the condom (if used) and throw it in the pail or flush it down the toilet. They then proceed to wash their genitals and towel drying before getting dressed. I have seen rapists who used a condom to prevent leaving semen in the victim, only to throw it out in the garbage pail! In addition, the towel often contains male DNA after washing. The investigator has to make a conscious effort to retrieve these items and submit them for proper testing. Investigators can run into a roadblock at any crime scene, but especially where a sexual assault occurred. Since the victim and perpetrator often know each other, the question will arise, "did he live or frequently stay at the location?" If so, most evidence you find in the bed or on clothes can easily be explained away by a defense attorney. "Of course you found pubic hairs in the bed. My client has been living there for over a year and a half!" However, investigators must apply inclusiveness when processing a crime scene.

DNA tests results can provide the following information for investigators:

1. No DNA evidence was recovered (or only from the victim)
2. DNA evidence revealed a male (or several) donor(s) that is/are not in CODIS
3. DNA evidence revealed a male (or several) donor(s) that is/are in CODIS

The first result is an investigator's worst nightmare, but there is nothing they can do but continue the investigation. Even though DNA was not recovered does not mean a rape did not occur. The suspect could have used a condom or did not ejaculate inside of the victim. This is why getting the victim to the hospital is extremely important. The sexual offense collection kit not only takes DNA swabs, but also the following: fingernail scrapings, pubic hair combings, and the victim's clothing.

A DNA hit, whether it is or isn't in CODIS, provides probable cause to arrest. However, the investigator will employ several investigative steps prior to arresting the suspect in hopes of getting a confession. Let's test what you learned so far. Take a piece of paper and write down some investigative steps. If possible, do not look at the steps that I would take below. The question is, "What would you do if you were the case investigator?" Here is a sampling of investigative steps that need to be taken:

- Make the victim feel safe and secure
- Establish a timeline of events of the victim for the past 24-48 hours
- Complete a victimology on the victim
- Conduct a thorough background check on the suspect paying special attention to previous brushes with the law
  - o   Active warrants?
  - o   Domestic violence complaints
  - o   Registered sex offender?
- Place a photo of the suspect in an array to show the victim(s) (if a stranger)
  - o   A single confirmatory photo can be shown to the victim in cases where the perpetrator is known to the victim
- Establish a record of the suspect's whereabouts on the date in question
- Surreptitiously obtain a DNA exemplar
- Interview former girlfriends and wives
- Can the person be matched to fingerprints left at the scene

Old rape cases make for good cold case investigations as long as the evidence can be located and tested. Finding the evidence from the case isn't the only problem. How they were packaged is another problem altogether. Before the law enforcement community learned about DNA, just about everything was vouchered in plastic. We now know that plastic degrades and destroys DNA evidence because of moisture build up inside of the packaging. Now, all evidence that can possibly contain DNA evidence is stored in brown paper bags. Lastly, many states have a statute of limitations for the prosecution of most crimes, except for murder.

If the investigator obtains a DNA profile, but a male donor cannot be identified in CODIS, the investigator will bring the "profile" to the district attorney's office. The ADA will determine if the case will be presented to a Grand Jury for a "John Doe" indictment. This is good and bad for investigators. A "John Doe" indictment stops the clock on the statue of limitations. This is good because a profile can be entered into CODIS and you may get the hit years later. A statute of limitations places a time frame on when a crime can be prosecuted. A "John Doe" indictment stops that statute. The flip side of a obtaining an indictment on the UNSUB, unknown subject, is that an indictment is an accusatory instrument. If you remember from Chapter 7: Interview and Interrogation, once an accusatory instrument has been filed, the subject, whoever it may be, will have an absolute right to counsel. That means the police cannot talk to him without the lawyer present. Good luck getting a confession.

Questions for Discussion and Review:

1. What type of packaging should be used for items with body fluids on them? Why?

2. In 66% of all rapes the victim knew their attacker. Explain why there is only a 40% arrest clearance rate?

3. Why does the public often place blame on the victim and not the perpetrator?

4. What role can a victimology play in a rape investigation?

5. Why would an active warrant on an unrelated matter be a possible "gift" for investigators? Explain your answer.

6. What type of information could an investigator obtain from an old girlfriend(s) or wife?

7. Do rapists participate in lesser crimes before "graduating" to rape? If so, what types of crimes?

8. What kind of water is used with swabs?

9. What role can bite mark evidence play in rape cases?

Robbery

"You get much further with a kind word and a gun, than you can with a kind word alone."
— Alphonse Capone

The FBI UCR (2009) defines robbery as the taking or attempting to take anything of value from a person by force or threat of force. In simple terms, robbery is the forcible taking of property from another. The use of force must be imminent and it can be used, simulated, implied or threatened. The victim must feel compelled to hand over their property or risk being hurt by the **FIST**:

Forcibly take property
Imminent
Simulated, implied, used or
Threatened use of force

According to the most recent FBI UCR (2009) Robbery statistics:

- There were 408,217 reported robberies in the United States in 2009
- Firearms were the choice of weapon 42.6 percent of the time
- Strong arm robberies accounted for 41.1 percent
- 42.8 percent of all robberies occurred on the street
- 28.2 percent of all robberies are cleared by arrest – therefore 74.1 percent of all robbers are still out there
- Every 1.2 minutes a person is robbed in the United States

Robberies occur so often that most investigative units have individuals assigned to do only robbery investigations. The key to solving robberies is to arrive at the scene as fast as possible and convince the victim to canvass for the perpetrator(s). Robbery investigations are usually "hot," meaning they just occurred. The investigator's skill in communication must persuade the victim to cooperate and follow through with the investigation. The victim's memory clock is ticking.

The longer the investigator waits or has to convince the person, the greater the chance the victim will not be able to identify the perpetrator. Many people "don't have the time," "glad they weren't hurt," "have to go to work" or they "have to run to pick up the children." The ten dollars that was stolen is "no big deal."

If the victim does not see anyone on the canvass, the investigator will immediately take them to the precinct to look at photos. This can be time consuming. So investigators will try to make it as easy as possible for the victim. Investigators can make arrangements to have the victim's children picked up at school, buy pizza so they don't have to worry about dinner all in an effort to secure their cooperation.

Investigating Robberies

Two key factors that will determine if a robbery case is solvable are:

(1) if the victim is able to pick out the suspect from photos
(2) if the property stolen is traceable.

Most robberies are a blitz style attack on some unsuspecting person and are usually from behind. In those instances, eyewitness identification will be impossible. Even if the victim had an opportunity to see the perpetrator, they still may not be unable to identify the perpetrator because of fear. In those instances, the investigator will ask, "Tell me about the person who robbed you," and the response will be, "He had a silver gun." "Was he White? Black? Or Hispanic?" "He had a silver gun." Tunnel vision is quite evident in victims of robbery. In addition, robbery perpetrators sometimes use a mask or other device (stocking, bandana, etc.) to change their appearance or avoid identification. Investigators must ask the victim if the suspect was wearing any of these types of items and pass that information along to the evidence collection team. These items may contain DNA from the suspect(s).

Eyewitness identification procedures were covered at length in Chapter 5, so I will concentrate on traceable property in this section. If the suspect is unable to identify the perpetrator, investigators must track down the property.

However, two problems exist for investigators:

(1) If the perpetrator took cash during the robbery, with the exception of a bank robbery, it will not be traceable
(2) when investigators locate the property and it is in the possession of an individual, does it mean that it is the person who robbed (took) it? No. In this scenario you would have at best a criminal possession of stolen property charge. But, that individual will be a possible link to the person who originally stole the property.

Traceable property is any property that can be tracked via the nature of the item: i.e., cell phone, credit card, debit card, ATM card, bus pass, or subway/train pass. The items most likely to be stolen fall under Ronald Clarke's **CRAVED** model (Clarke, 1999, p. 28).

Concealable
Removable
Available
Valuable
Enjoyable
Disposable

The items most likely to fall under just about every category in Clarke's model are small electronic devices. These items are often the target of the youthful robbery offender. Eventually, the property is going to end up somewhere when the person needs money or is tired of using it. Where an investigator looks depends on the type of property that was stolen. Investigators attempt to investigate backwards: Find the property to find the perpetrator. Here is a sampling of where stolen property can show up:

Jewelry = Pawnshop
Small electronic devices = online auction and social networking sites

Jewelry, such as watches, necklaces and rings can be turned into immediate cash through local pawnshops. However, over the past decade or so, local governments have exerted pressure on these types of businesses and have established administrative rules for second hand dealers, AKA pawnshops. Many states now require second hand dealers to photocopy identification of individuals selling items as well as keep a log. Investigators will peruse these logs in the hopes of identify suspects from past robberies. A new trend for dealing with pawnshops is the requirement of second hand dealers to take digital photographs of the property and upload them to an online site for law enforcement to use. This aids law enforcement in not only identifying suspects but recovering stolen property as well.

Obtaining an accurate description of the jewelry is important. Victims may have it insured and therefore have pictures of it or in cases with unique jewelry; an investigator can use the services of a sketch artist. The sketches can be made into flyers and given to the pawnshop owners so they can be on the look out for it.

The Internet has created other opportunities for perpetrators to cash in on their ill gotten goods, by listing and selling the items on the World Wide Web. Victims also know this and often find their own items for sale on the Web and notify the police. Investigators must obtain a subpoena for seller/buyer information.

Investigators have seen a new trend with the Internet: social networking and video sites. More and more investigators are finding themselves trolling the Net for information about crime and criminals. Whether it is a "how-to video" or the video recording of the actual robbery, both can be obtained without a warrant. No one has a right to privacy about anything they put on the Net.

The investigator must convince the victim not to cancel their service (cell phone, credit card, bus pass etc.), so the police can investigate it in "real" time. Police departments have funds that are used to keep the account open. Once a bank or cell phone company is on board with the investigation, they can notify the police of when and where the item is being used. If investigators are lucky enough to arrive at the scene when the perpetrator is still there, great, but if they can't, an immediate request for video surveillance footage will be made. Investigators must get into the habit of requesting two copies of the tape whenever possible. One will be vouchered and kept with the case folder and the other will be used for viewing purposes. This prevents the destruction and/or inadvertent loss of the video evidence. Investigators must act quickly to secure surveillance evidence. Some recording devices will re-record over old footage after a certain number of hours.

Cell phones offer a unique way to track individuals wanted for serious crimes. Each cellular device is connected to a satellite through cell towers. When the devices are used, they connect to the nearest cell tower. These towers can track down the actual location of the phone within a few feet. Investigators must be on standby and be able to respond to a location at any given notice. This electronic surveillance measure is called a Pen Register Trap and Trace. Law enforcement officials need to obtain a warrant from a judge, by establishing probable cause and filing an affidavit.

Cell phones offer additional information as to who the robber is. Investigators will subpoena the phone records from the time of the robbery forward. You wouldn't believe how many thieves call someone they know after stealing the device!

Robberies occur in the street more than any place else. So an investigator must reach out to the street for answers. A canvass for surveillance cameras can be fruitful, but investigators place a greater value on human intelligence or HUMINT, in the form of confidential informants (CI). The rules about using CIs were discussed in Chapter 5, so I am going to discuss the pros and cons of using CIs in this section. Remember, the investigator must conduct background checks on potential informants and always identify the motive of the person before they sign them up as a confidential informant! CIs can play a pivotal role in solving many of the 8 Major crimes, as well as provide information on narcotics and gang activities. The investigator will always keep in mind the value of obtaining an informant when investigating any case.

The use of confidential informants (CIs) has both pros and cons for an investigator.

The pros of using a CI are to **SEW** the pieces of the puzzle together:

Street knowledge
Exactly where to find your suspect
Wear a wire or introduce a police undercover

Street knowledge

Many perpetrators use robberies to support their drug habit. So much of what the investigator needs to know comes from the street. CIs live on the street and many times are drug users themselves. They know who is doing it, where they operate and what they like to do. Investigators call this the Modus Operandi or method of operation. A unique MO in robbery cases can help in establishing a pattern. A pattern is two (2) or more crimes with similar MOs or likenesses.

Exactly where to find your suspect

Investigators spend a lot of time tracking the whereabouts of their suspect. These efforts can be exhausting when challenged by an experienced perpetrator who is on the run. CIs know where they hang out, what apartment they live in or where their girlfriends lives. Investigators are often faced with information that a suspect is hiding out in a certain building, only to find that there are over 500 apartments! Good CIs know how to find out this type of information. Accurate and timely information is worth the money. CIs can be in constant contact with new technology with the use of cell phones and text messages by providing an accurate description of what the suspect is wearing and exactly where they are standing.

Wear a wire or introduce a police undercover

A wire worn by a CI can provide evidence that is invaluable. An admission or even a confession on tape will be the words that seal a suspect's fate. A wire can be used to dismantle robbery, auto theft and burglary rings as well as narcotic operations. If the informant does not want to wear a wire or wearing one would be too dangerous, the informant can try and introduce a police undercover into the operation. This technique has been successful investigating organized crime cases in the past.

The cons of using a CI are sometimes a **LAST** resort:

Lie to keep the money coming in
Addicts
Sometimes not reliable
Trouble

Lie to keep the money coming in

An informant knows that if he/she provides information, they get paid. Some will play the system, "I keep talking, and they'll keep paying." Investigators must corroborate the information that is received so the police department doesn't get ripped off.

Addicts

When a CI is or was a drug user, their credibility is tainted. For this reason, some jurisdictions may disqualify someone from being a CI.

Sometimes not reliable

CIs live and operate in the street which makes it difficult to find them. Couple this with drug use and the investigator has the makings of a disaster. CIs have also been known to play the role of double agent, so investigators must not reveal pertinent information about themselves or the case.

Trouble

The next time a CI gets into trouble with the law, who do you think he/she is going to call? Yes, the investigator that is using them as a CI. Many informants think that providing information for money to the police is a get out of jail free card. Many will sign up with this exact thought in mind.

Computer checks can also provide the information that an investigator can use to solve robbery cases and establish patterns. Sometimes suspects are arrested in other jurisdictions for similar crimes. This may present itself as the needed break in the case. Searching through Stop, Question and Frisk reports to match descriptions against your perpetrator or to identify persons who where stopped in the vicinity of reported robbery occurrences are also good starting points. The same checks can be done for criminal court summonses. At the very least, this information can pinpoint where the suspect likes to hang out or lay their head.

A robbery is a crime that plagues many of societies today. Because of the blitz style attack, many of the perpetrators are never caught, so investigators have to deal with what they have. Conducting the proper canvasses, computer checks and tracking down property are the best methods to identify and apprehend robbery perpetrators.

Questions for Discussion and Review:

1. Johnny Jones walks up to Sammy Smith and states, "If you don't give me that MP3 player I am going to burn down your house next week." If caught, would Johnny be charged with robbery? Why or why not?

2. In your opinion, what crime do you think the general public fears the most and why?

3. What eyewitness identification method(s) would be used to identify robbery perpetrators?

4. Why are robbery cases so difficult to solve? Explain your answer.

5. List some similarities in robbery case that can lead to the development of a robbery pattern.

Felony (Aggravated) Assault

The FBI's 2009 Uniform Crime Report defines Aggravated Assault as an unlawful attack by one person on another with the purpose of inflicting severe or aggravated bodily injury. In simpler terms, you intend to cause a serious physical injury to another person and you do so or you cause any injury (however slight) with a deadly weapon or dangerous instrument. A serious physical injury (SPI) can cause protracted health issues and or death of the victim. Examples of serious physical injuries are stab wounds, gunshot wounds and broken bones. Remember, only people can be assaulted. Aggravated assault is always a felony, but it must be distinguished from a simple assault. This is why it is commonly referred to as Felony Assault and will be throughout the rest of this chapter.

Felony assault has a little brother, his name is simple Assault. Simple Assault is always a misdemeanor and occurs when one individual causes a physical injury (PI) to another. Examples of physical injuries are: a black eye, bloody lip, broken nose and various other types of bruising. If no physical injury occurs, or a physical injury is not visible, it is a violation known as Harassment. Violations are not enforceable by the police unless it happens in their presence (exceptions in domestic violence cases).

Most jurisdictions recognize nine (9) deadly weapons (DW). The mere possession of these weapons is an automatic felony charge and no intent to use the weapon must be proved. The nature of these weapons are to assault, kill or maim. They serve no other useful or lawful purpose and it doesn't matter how big/small they are. "This switchblade is less than four inches." It doesn't matter, it's a felony. If they are used in a felonious assault, the perpetrator will also be charged with a felony criminal possession of a weapon in addition to the felony assault charge.

The nine (9) most common deadly weapons are:

1. Loaded, operable firearm
2. Ballistic Knife
3. Dagger
4. Switchblade
5. Gravity Knife
6. Metal Knuckle Knife
7. Metal Knuckles
8. Billy Club
9. Blackjack

Any item that does not fit in the above categories is classified as a dangerous instrument (DI). Dangerous instruments have a useful or lawful purpose and the police and prosecution have to show intent in order to charge someone with criminal possession of a weapon. For example, carrying a pencil in your pocket is not a crime, but if it is used to stick someone in the eye, then it becomes a dangerous instrument.

Fast facts about Felony Assault from the 2009 UCR:

- There were 806,843 aggravated assaults reported in the U.S.
- 56.8% of aggravated assaults were closed by arrest
- There is an aggravated assault in the U.S. every 36.8 seconds
- A weapon of opportunity is the most used during felony assaults, followed by firearms

---

CI Tip Sheet

Here is a quick reminder on when someone would be charged with Felony Assault (varying degrees):

PI + DW/DI = Felony Assault
SPI = Felony Assault
SPI + DW/DI = Felony Assault

The most likely felony assault an investigator will "catch" is a non-fatal shooting/stabbing. Remember, the charge is not attempted murder but felony assault—even though the perpetrator's intent was to kill them. Non-fatal shootings/stabbings are also the most likely to cause the investigator a headache. Some of your victims will not be cooperative in the investigation. This spells trouble. Instead, your victim will be thinking about taking care of it themselves through an act of revenge. This revenge can be extracted against the perpetrator or one of their "crew." Investigators have to work hard and fast to identify and arrest the perpetrator or there will be a murder or an additional non-fatal shooting/stabbing. The role of investigators here is to stop the violence from spreading.

Here are some investigative techniques that may be used in a Felony Assault investigation:

The hardest part of a felony assault investigation is to prove the element of intent, establish the extent of the victim's injury and identify the type of weapon used in the attack. Since many shootings and stabbings occur inside/outside of a licensed premises (bar, nightclub, pool hall, etc.), the investigator could do the following:

- Ask for Surveillance camera footage
- A list of patrons (many bars scan driver's licenses at the front door)
- Conduct a hospital canvass for additional victims and potential witnesses
- Prompt on the scene interviews with witnesses
  - o Including the entire bar staff
    - Wait staff, bartenders, cooks, bar backs, etc.
- Request a license plate reader to "collect" the plate numbers of vehicles parked in close proximity of the location

If video surveillance does not exist, investigators must rely on victim and witness statements. This can become a problem when assaults happen in nightclubs or bars. Many of your witnesses, including your witness have more than likely been drinking. This presents another obstacle that investigators must overcome.

Questions for Discussion and Review

1. In order to have a felony assault, what must there be?

2. After a "Weapon of Opportunity," what is the most likely used weapon in a felony assault?

3. What is the difference between a physical injury (PI) and a serious physical injury (SPI)?

4. What type of felony assault is an investigator likely to catch? Why?

5. Describe the difference between a deadly weapon (DW) and a dangerous instrument (DI).

Chapter 10

Crimes Against Property

Burglary

"We've basically built doors for 4,000 years and still have burglaries."

— Johannes Ullrich

When mentioned on the news or in passing, the crime of burglary is often confused with robbery. It has been noted earlier that the definition of robbery is the forcible stealing of property. How many times have you heard the following, "My house was robbed!" A quick reminder: people get robbed, houses get burglarized.

In order to commit the crime of burglary, certain elements must be present: The perpetrator must be a **BIKER**:

Building
Intent to commit a crime therein
Knowingly
Enter or
Remain unlawfully

Building

A building is defined as any walled and roofed structure that is used for overnight lodging or to conduct business out of. The definition of a building would include dwellings, vessels, trailers, hotels, motels, RVs and stores to name a few. These locations can either be locked, unlocked or abandoned.

Intent to commit a crime therein

The individual who enters the building must have the intent to commit a crime - it doesn't have to be a felony. This is the essential element of the crime of Burglary. A burglar enters a home for a reason, cash, jewelry or any item that can be turned into cash. The rationale behind almost all burglaries is to commit some sort of larceny. Ironically, the perpetrator does not actually have to remove any property.

Knowingly

This is a self-explanatory culpable mental state. The individual knows they don't live or work at the location and shouldn't be there.

Enter or

The individual actually has to gain access to the building, if not they could be charged with attempted burglary. They don't have to break in; walking into an open door is good enough.

Remain unlawfully

The individual inside of the house was not invited in by the owner. For instance, you are invited to a friend's house for a Christmas party. You go to the room where everyone puts their coats and you see a pocketbook on the nightstand. You look around, reach in and remove $100 in cash from the purse and stuff it in your pocket. If caught, you would not be charged with burglary because you were there lawfully and you did not have the initial intent to commit a crime therein, it was an afterthought.

According to the 2009 report by the FBI, *Crime in the United States*, a burglary occurs in the United States every 14.5 seconds to the tune of over 2 million a year. It also has the lowest clearance rate, 12.5%, of the 8 Major Felonies. That means 87.6% of all burglars are walking around and living in our neighborhoods! Of the 2 million burglaries that occur every year, nearly 68% of them are committed against home-owners. This is why many police departments across the country have turned to crime prevention techniques to help stem the tide of burglaries. One reason burglaries go unsolved is since there are so many burglaries, police departments cannot afford to send a crime scene unit out to every reported burglary. It is either left up to the patrol officer to conduct a preliminary investigation or send in the evidence collection team. Unless someone is caught in the act, leaves prints and/or DNA behind, it is extremely difficult to identify and arrest the perpetrator(s).

Burglary Fast Facts:

- #1 burglar method to get into a home is by forcing their way through the front door
- #1 burglar method to get into a commercial establishment is through a back door at night
- A forcible entry into the location is not necessary to be charged with burglary
- Most burglaries occur during the day time when people are at work
- Busiest months for burglary are during the summer, when people are on vacation
- Burglary is always a felony
- Depending on what jurisdiction you live in, the classification of felony may differ
- If the burglar is armed with a deadly weapon and enters a dwelling, a higher class of felony would be charged
- Burglary does have a younger brother, his name is Criminal Trespass
    - You commit the crime of criminal trespass when you enter upon fenced land or in a building (no intent to commit a crime) – it is the acronym BIKER without the I

Entry points into the location must be given the most attention in burglary investigations. Burglars are in such a hurry to get into the place that they often leave behind physical evidence, fingerprints or DNA. Here are some other investigative techniques that might be used during a burglary investigation:

- Check the location for past calls for police services
    - Suspicious person(s)
- Was anyone stopped at or near the scene?
    - Check Stop and Frisk database
- Canvass of the neighborhood should be made for information

- Check police computer databases for recently released burglars residing in your jurisdiction
- Check for possible surveillance video - even in residential neighborhoods
- Interview the homeowner
  o Ask owner if anything has been moved or touched
    - Have location or item dusted
  o Any victimization of burglary in the past?
  o What do they do for a living?
- Was any property taken traceable?
  o Coin collections
  o Unique jewelry
    - Think of using a sketch artist to draw unique jewelry
  o Credit cards
  o Cell phones
  o Follow up on the property with local pawn shops and Internet sites
- Attempt to drill down to the exact time of the occurrence
- Identify patterns by time, place and MO
- Entry and exit points should be "dusted" for fingerprints and/or swabbed for DNA - especially walls by a window
  o Take elimination prints/swabs from residents
- Tool marks may exist at entry/exit points - try to take the entire mark as evidence

Questions for Discussion and Review:

1. If Johnny Jones enters an opened mausoleum with the intent to steal something from inside and is caught, what crime will the police charge him with?

2. Johnny Jones is out the next day and sees a parked, unattended ice cream truck on the side of the road. He breaks the window and takes a fudge pop. If caught what crime would Johnny be charged with?

3. Mary Smith is homeless and breaks into the backdoor of a factory to get warm and shelter from the cold. The police are called and they arrest her. What is the charge?

4. A car belonging to the phone company is parked in front of building during a maintenance call at a residence. Johnny Jones reaches through a slightly opened window and removes a telephone handset. He is apprehended on the spot. What crime would he be charged with?

5. Why do burglars choose rear doors in commercial establishments at night?

6. Johnny Jones knocks on the door of someone's home. Mary Smith opens the door and Johnny forces his way in. He punches and ties Mary up to a chair. He then proceeds to ransack the house, taking money and jewelry. If Johnny is caught, what crime(s) would he be charged with?

Grand Larceny and Grand Larceny Auto (GLA)

The FBI's UCR defines larceny as the taking of property from another, *without force*. Remember, if any force is used or threatened the crime would be a Robbery. Since larcenies occur at such a high rate, cities across the U.S. report a category of Grand Larceny for UCR reporting purposes that sets a dollar amount or action surrounding the crime. For example, in New York State* there are many ways to commit Grand Larceny, but the three most likely are:

1. Take property valued over $1,000 - i.e., $1,000.01
2. Take someone's credit card/debit card - possession alone
    a. Having the numbers is good enough
3. Theft from the person - i.e., chain or purse snatch, pickpocket
    a. No force: Force = Robbery

For example, Johnny Jones is walking down the street with a knife in his pocket. He sees an older woman walking down the street with a pocketbook dangling from her forearm. He runs up behind her and cuts the straps of her pocketbook, grabs it and runs in the opposite direction. The crime in this scenario is a Grand Larceny.

CI Cheat Sheet

Force = Robbery

---

*Each jurisdiction may be different

Fast Facts about Larceny from the FBI's 2009 UCR:

-   Larceny is the most popular type of property crime
-   There were over 6.3 million larcenies in the U.S. in 2009
-   21.5% of all larcenies are cleared by arrest
-   There is a larceny every 4.8 seconds in the U.S.

Most Grand Larcenies have to deal with some type of physical property so investigators must first look at the locations where stolen items can be "fenced." Crime analysis, the collection of data and crime statistics, may help put together patterns of larcenies in a specific geographic area. The location and times when these crimes are committed may provide the lead necessary to solve the case. However, without a good description, investigators face the same problems as they do in robbery investigations.

- Pawnshops, second hand jewelers, online auction sites provide the perpetrators an avenue to sell their stolen goods. To learn more about how an investigator can use these avenues, see the Robbery section in Chapter 8.

- Identify any "Traceable Property," cell phones, credit cards, etc., and try to investigate them in real time. Especially in cases with credit cards. Banks and credit card companies can keep the account open and report where and when the card was last used. If the event is in the past, the investigator must respond to the location as fast as they can in order to obtain video surveillance footage.

- Decoy operations are also an option for investigators, but do pose a threat to the safety of the decoy officer and to the general public.

Grand Larceny Auto (GLA)

The FBI's UCR defines Motor Vehicle Theft as the theft or attempted theft of an automobile without the owner's consent. An automobile is something that is used on land, is not on rails and is self-propelled. Anything that uses human power to move, i.e., bicycle, is not considered a motor vehicle.

Fast Facts from the FBI's 2009 UCR for GLA:

- There were 794,616 automobiles stolen in the U.S.
- A motor vehicle is stolen every 28.8 seconds in the U.S.
- Only 12.4% of all GLAs are closed through arrest
  o Second lowest behind burglary (12.5%)

Motor vehicles are stolen from the **Pure JOY** of **IT**.

Parts

The main reason why a vehicle is stolen is for the parts. The parts are more valuable then the "whole" motor vehicle. The thief often is provided a shopping list of vehicles to steal. Chop shops are locations where stolen cars are brought so that parts can be "surgically" removed to be resold to unsuspecting customers at full price. These parts end up for sale through several routes including classified ads, trade shows and online auctions.

JOYriding

Joyriding is generally done by juveniles for fun and excitement. Joyriding juveniles target fancy cars that would be fun to drive. These autos are generally left within the vicinity after the kids got bored (or scared) of driving it.

Insurance Fraud

Insurance fraud is another problem for investigators as owner's stage the crime to look like a GLA. Many times the owner does not do a good job. Many police departments have initiated a preliminary theft report that requires the owner to make a full written statement of the event with the intent on charging them with Filing a False Report if it is determined that they lied. In an economic downturn, like we are experiencing now, the investigator will see a rise in auto thefts. Many of them will turn out to be insurance fraud.

Transportation

People steal cars just to go home or work. My experience has told me that Friday and Saturday nights are popular for these types of incidents. Why take a train or a cab home?

The theft of a single automobile will rarely spark an investigation unless it is part of a pattern or organized ring. Generally, auto theft cases will be closed by patrol officers during their preliminary investigation and therefore hold very little significance to investigators.

Arson

> *"It's arson. There's no lights, no electricity and no gas. What else is going to start it?"*
>
> — Jay Lewis

The crime of Arson is defined by the FBI's UCR as the willful burning of house, vehicle or other personal property of another. As stated earlier, the New York City Police Department is one of the agencies that does not report the crime of Arson to the FBI for UCR statistics. According to the UCR, about one-third of police agencies do not report Arson, probably because the number of reported incidents is quite small compared to the other Major Crimes.

2001 Fast facts about arson from the United States Fire Administration:

- Arson is the leading cause of fire in the U.S.
- There were over 267,000 crimes of arson in the U.S.
- Arson was responsible for 475 deaths
- Half of all arrests for arson are juveniles
- 20% of all arson complaints are on vehicles
- 30% of all arson complaints are on structures
- Arsons peak on specific days: New Year's, July 4 and Halloween

Due to the nature of the crime, arson investigations are extremely difficult. Whatever physical evidence of the crime was not destroyed by the fire is often destroyed inadvertently by the fire personnel while putting it out. Water, foam, axes and other equipment used to suppress the fire also has a harmful affect on evidence. Arson investigations are conducted by investigators in both the police and fire departments. In most cases, because it is a crime scene, police personnel generally take the lead in the investigation and are supported by their fire brethren.

To warrant an arson investigation, there must be some evidence discovered at the scene. Examples of evidence could be an accelerant residue, an unusual point of origin such as the living room, or an unusual amount of one type of material such as newspapers or wood. Arson investigations usually kick off when a body is found at the scene of a fire and an autopsy reveals that the manner of death is homicide. Fire scenes where a body is found should be treated like a crime scene and held until the medical examiner determines the manner of death. Investigators will initially have an "Emergency Exception" for a search warrant so that they can secure evidence of the crime before it is destroyed. However, once the evidence can be located in the fire scene, investigators will need to obtain a warrant for the location.

Arson is a crime of choice by individuals who like to roll the **DICE**:

> **D**estroy evidence of another crime (i.e., murder, rape, etc.)
> **I**nsurance Fraud
> **C**ompetitors in business
> **E**xcitement

Destroy evidence of another crime (i.e., murder, rape, etc.)

Perpetrators attempt to destroy evidence with fire. In most cases, it will destroy DNA and trace evidence, but not the body itself in homicide cases. An ordinary fire does not rise to the temperature level needed to "cremate" the body. According to the Cremation Association of America (2000), it takes temperatures of 1,400° to 1,800° to cremate a body and about 1½ to 3 hours depending on the size of the individual. Often, the body still can tell the story on how the person met his/her demise. Bullet holes in skulls or chip marks in bones are quite evident to pathologists, even after a fire. This is why it is imperative that patrol officers establish a crime scene to protect whatever evidence remains. This is the key in solving arson cases.

Insurance Fraud

When individuals can no longer afford a car payment or mortgage payment, they may resort to arson to relieve themselves of the financial burden. Unfortunately for them, evidence of arson is quite obvious. Investigators will search for records of an unexpected increase in insurance on the property as well as complete an extensive financial background investigation on the owner(s).

Competitors in business

Local business disputes can get ugly, quickly. Competitors use arson to knock out their competition, faster than product pricing. Investigators need to determine who would benefit from the fire and search police reports for any previous threats that were made to the owner.

Excitement

Arsonists set fires for the pure excitement of watching the fire grow and listening to the sirens. Also, arsonists use setting fires as a form of sexual gratification.

Questions for Discussion and Review:

1. Johnny walked up to Mary and stated, "If you don't give me your money, I'm going to burn down your house next week." If arrested, what crime would Johnny be charged with and why?

2. What types of products could be used as an accelerant?

3. Why is the point of origin so important to investigators?

Chapter 11

Trial Preparation

What Court Am I Going to?

In general, all arrested persons go to a local criminal court where they are booked and arraigned. At arraignment, the judge may dispose of the case, release the individual on their own recognizance (ROR), impose bail, or remand the person for trial. Depending on the crime category, misdemeanor or felony depends on what court the individual will go to. Misdemeanors will stay at the criminal court level, but felony cases will be sent over to the local Supreme Court for Grand Jury. Trials are a very rare occurrence. Most cases are plea bargained. Only in television would you have a crime, an investigation and a trial in 45 minutes with three commercials.

A grand jury is composed of 16-23 citizens whose function is to listen to the investigator's and the prosecutor's details of the case and decide if there is enough evidence to move forward. Judge input, defense attorneys and witnesses are generally absent from a Grand Jury. It is often viewed as an arm of the prosecutor's office. The grand jury will convene and vote to pass down a true bill, also known as an indictment. This is where the old saying came from, "You can indict a ham sandwich," because the process is seen as one sided.

Let the games begin! As the investigator prepares for their first trial, they should be aware of the general process that takes place. The two (2) main actors in the courtroom are the defense attorney and the prosecutor. The investigator prepares for the trial by reviewing the case folder, their notes, lab reports, photos, videos etc. At some point in time you sill sit down with the prosecutor who will prep you for the trial by going over evidence procedures, interviews or interrogations that were conducted or any other pertinent material.

The investigator has to look and act the part. Think of testifying like you were preparing to walk out onto a big stage. Male investigators are required to wear proper business attire encompassing a suit, shirt with a collar and tie. Female investigators are required to wear a business suit or dress.

Courtroom testimony for the police is essentially the same for any type of case. Whether it is for a felony drug collar or a petit larceny, the investigator's integrity, appearance, demeanor and credibility are paramount under cross-examination. Don't believe me? The next trial you see on television, just look at the defendant. You wouldn't recognize him. They have been cleaned up, their hair has been cut and they are wearing business attire. The defense understands that appearance plays an important role, so should the investigator.

The investigator's personal appearance plays an integral part of the pretrial preparation. Their actions make up the rest. Inappropriate behavior, like fooling around, inside or outside of the courtroom can sink the officer before they even take the stand. When they sit in the witness box their feet are planted firmly on the floor, hands on their knees and will sit upright. Leaning back in the chair perceives the officer as cocky and overconfident. The officer must look at the attorney when they are asked a question and to the jury when they answer it. Remember, actions speak louder than words.

Testifying in a courtroom is similar to writing a research paper – there is an introduction, a body and a conclusion. Investigative steps need to be broken down into their simplest terms so that it can be followed as a sequence of events. A blow-by-blow description of the circumstances and events that led up to the investigator taking the person into custody should be carefully followed. The investigator, like the student, must put into words all of the things that they felt, found and witnessed.

Pre-Trial Hearings

Before a trial starts, the investigator may have to testify in what are called suppression hearings. A Mapp Hearing (*Mapp v. Ohio*, 367 U.S. 643 (1960) is a hearing that determines the admissibility of evidence BEFORE the jury is told that it exists. For example, a murder weapon will not be brought into the courtroom until a judge decides before the trial if it will be admissible.

A Wade Hearing (*United States v. Wade*, 388 US 218 (1967)) will determine what witnesses can testify and what they can testify about. For example a judge may not allow a witness to testify about the lineup, but will allow them to discuss other events.

The Culpable Mental States

A perpetrator who commits an offense has criminal liability. They can only commit a crime in four (4) ways, known as the culpable mental states or what the person was thinking or not thinking at the time the offense was committed. Culpable mental states play an important role in charging perpetrators with a criminal offense. For instance, *intentional* murder (premeditation) is a higher charge than criminally negligent homicide. This task falls on the prosecutor.

The culpable mental states can be remembered by using **RICK**:

Recklessly
Intentionally
Criminal Negligence
Knowingly

Recklessly

A person perceives the risk, but disregards it. (A person practicing swinging a baseball bat near a crowd of people)

Intentionally

The person meant to do the crime and did it.

Criminal Negligence

The person fails to perceive a substantial risk. They are "super reckless." (A person drops a cinderblock off the highway overpass into oncoming traffic.)

Knowingly

The person who committed the crime is aware that their actions are illegal.

Defenses: It Wasn't Me

The number one phrase probably used by the bad guys is, "It wasn't me." A defense must be raised by the defendant and disproved by the PROSECUTION (District Attorney's Office) Beyond a Reasonable Doubt. Beyond a Reasonable Doubt means that no questions can be raised of the person's innocence; they did it.

The two defenses that must be raised at the time of trial by the defense are Infancy and Justification.

Infancy is the person was too young, usually less than 16 years of age. However, if a juvenile less than sixteen commits certain felonies such as: Murder, Manslaughter, Rape, Sodomy, Kidnapping, Robbery, Burglary and Criminal Possession of a Weapon, they will be treated as Juvenile Offenders and be tried as an adult in most jurisdictions.

The term Justification is what under a normal situation the actions by the defendant would constitute a crime. However, if the defendant was using physical force required and authorized by law or judicial decree then it is justified. Or such action was necessary to prevent, terminate or make an arrest for a crime. This is the defense that protects police officers during the course of their duties and also ordinary citizens. For instance a police officer shoots and kills an individual that was using deadly physical force against another person. This would be classified as a justifiable homicide.

Affirmative Defenses are raised by the defendant and must be proved by the DEFENSE with a Preponderance of the Evidence. Preponderance of the Evidence means the defense has raised more evidence that his client didn't commit the crime or 51% for the defense and 49% for the prosecution.

There are four (4) Affirmative Defenses which can be easily remembered by using the acronym **DR ME**:

Duress
Renunciation

Mental defect
Entrapment

Duress

The defendant was coerced or forced to do the crime because of imminent use of physical force against him or a third person. A perpetrator grabs your son, puts a knife to his throat and says "If you don't set that building on fire across the street, I'm going to kill your son." You believe that the perpetrator will hurt your son, so you do it.

Renunciation

The defendant, prior to the commission of a felony, changed his mind and attempted to prevent that felony from occurring. An example of renunciation is as follows: two men walk into a liquor store with the intent of robbing the store. One of the perpetrators notices that an older woman is working alone and decides not to carry out the robbery. He grabs his buddy and attempts to leave. His friend refuses and robs the store anyway.

Mental defect

This is the famous insanity defense, which doesn't happen as much as you think. The defendant committed the crime but lacked the responsibility for his actions because of a mental defect or disease.

Entrapment

The defendant was induced or encouraged to do so by a public servant. The entrapment defense is used a lot in criminal trials involving the buying/selling of illegal narcotics and firearms to undercover police as well as prostitution stings.

Cross-Examination

The investigator will be cross-examined by the defense attorney. The defense will attempt to paint the investigator as sloppy and incompetent by "breaking them down." This is all in an effort to sow the seeds of doubt in the minds of the jury and be able to bring up all of the "mistakes" in their final summation—or closing argument. For example, you arrested an individual for murder where they shot and killed the victim during a robbery. The firearm and/or the money may never be recovered and the defense will design their questions so the investigator must testify that the defendant was apprehended without the firearm/money, so the "real" shooter is still out there. But the investigator shouldn't worry about this cross-examination tactic, because they will be able to explain to the jury when the prosecutor redirects. This is where the investigator will be able to explain the positive results of the gunshot residue testing that was conducted and testify about the video surveillance evidence that was recovered during the canvass, which captured the event on tape.

The investigator that knows how to testify, knows the case and knows what to expect, will cause the defense's case to be **WILTED** like a flower. The investigator must be prepared to testify about the following:

Weather

- Especially in outdoor crime scenes
  - o   Rainy/Sunny
  - o   Clear/Foggy
  - o   Sleet/Snow

Identity of other members of the police department that were on the scene

- Ensure that you have the "gatekeeper's" list (see Chapter 4)
- Patrol officers
- Supervisors
- Other members of the investigating unit

Layout of the crime scene (indoors/outdoors)

- Refer to the rough sketch you prepared (see Chapter 4)

Time the event(s) occurred

- Refer to the investigative timeline you created (Chapter 4)

Exact location of:

- The address of the crime scene or configuration of streets
- The physical/forensic evidence found at the crime scene
  - o If a search warrant was/was not obtained
- The body when it was found (homicide cases)

Description of the suspect(s) when they were apprehended

- Clothing worn
  - o Corroborate witness/victim statements and video surveillance
- Physical condition
  - o Cuts, scrapes, bruises, etc.

The Investigator Testifying in Court

- Always tell the truth
- The investigator will be thoroughly prepared before testifying in any court
  - o Review the case folder, notes and physical evidence
- Avoid using police jargon in your courtroom testimony. I know very few people that use the phrases: "I exited the vehicle," or "I entered the premises."
- If the investigator does not know the answer to the question he/she should respond, "I don't know," **not** "I don't recall"
- When asked, "Did you discuss the case with anyone?" Of course you did: the district attorney and fellow officers who were at the scene. The answer to this question is NEVER no!
- Ask for permission before reading directly from the case folder
- Do not use the word(s): perp, perpetrator, and suspect - refer to them as the defendant or by name or as Mr. or Mrs., etc.
- Do not answer questions before they are asked
- Answer only the questioned that is asked

- Do not constantly look at the Prosecutor for help during cross examination. This gives the impression the investigator is unprepared, unable to answer on his/her own or was coached
- Be careful of defense lawyer cross examination traps
  - Rapid fire questions
    - Slow them down - it's a trap
  - Asking "Yes" or "No" answers without allowing an explanation
  - Silent treatment
    - Human nature is to fill the dead space by talking, often too much
  - Baiting the investigator to lose his/her cool

References

Australian Museum. (2003). "Decomposition: what happens to the body after death," Retrieved on October 23, 2009. Retrieved from http://www.deathonline.net/decomposition/body_changes/grave_wax.htm

Center for Disease Control and Prevention (CDC). (2004) Suicide Statistics. Retrieved on March 10, 2009, from http://www.cdc.gov/ViolencePrevention/pdf/Suicide-DataSheet-a.pdf

Chisum, W. J. & Turvey, B. (2000). "Evidence dynamics: Locard's exchange principle and crime reconstruction" Journal of Behavioral Profiling, January, Retrieved on October 17, 2009, retrieved from: http://www.profiling.org/journal/vol1_no1/jbp_ed_january2000_1-1.html

Clarke, R. (1999). Hot products: anticipating and reducing demand for stolen goods. Police Research Paper 112, London, UK. Retrieved on April 12, 2009, from http://www.homeoffice.gov.uk/rds/prgpdfs/fprs112.pdf

Connors, E., Lundregan, T., Miller, N. & McEwen, T. (1996). Convicted by juries, exonerated by science: case studies in the use of DNA evidence to establish innocence after trial. Retrieved on April 14, 2009, from http://www.ncjrs.gov/pdffiles/dnaevid.pdf

Cremation Association of North America. (2000). The Cremation: Processing the Remains. Retrieved on July 30, 2009, from http://www.funeralplan.com/funeralplan/cremation/cremationprocessing.html

Cronin, J., Murphy, G., Spahr, L, Toliver, J., & Weger R. (2007). Promoting effective homicide investigations. Police Executive Research Forum, Washington D.C. Retrieved on 10/6/2008. from http://www.cops.usdoj.gov/files/ric/Publications/promoting%20effective%20homicide%20investigations.pdf

DiMaio, v. & DiMaio, D. (2001). Forensic pathology. CRC Press, Boca Raton, FL

DNA.gov (2009). DNA initiative: DNA.gov mitochondrial DNA. Retrieved on April 10, 2009, from http://www.dna.gov/ research/mitochondrial_research/

FBI. (2007). Uniform Crime Report (UCR): Crime in the United States. Retrieved on February 16, 2009, from http://www. fbi/gov/ucr/cius2007/index.html

Gaines, P. (2009). Remember: A Rod has never taken steroids: according to A-Rod. Deadspin.com. Retrieved on April 9, 2009, from http://deadspin.com/5148732/remember- a+rod-has-never-taken-steroids-according-to-a+rod

Giacalone, J. (2006). Writing crime New York style: Miranda. Retrieved on March 31, 2009, from http://www.writing. com/main/view_item/item_id/822133

Giacalone, J. (2009). Five types of canvasses made easy. Private Investigator Magazine. March/April

Hall, R. (n.d.) "Suicide Risk Assessment: A Review of Risk Factors For Suicide In 100 Patients Who Made Severe Suicide Attempts." retrieved on October 17, 2009, retrieved from http://www.drrichardhall.com/suicide.htm

Japan Times Online. "Young teen suicides up 22.7% in 2006" June 8, 2007

Kirk, P.L., (1974). Crime Investigation, 2nd ed., New York: John Wiley & Sons, Inc.

National Institute of Justice. (2003). "What every law enforce- ment officer should know about DNA," Issue 249, July

New York State Criminal Procedural Law (CPL)

Newsday (2009). Supreme Court limits warrantless vehicle search. April 22, 2009.

Nolte, K., Hanzlick, R., Payne, D., Kroger, A., Oliver, W., Baker, A. et al. (2004). Medical Examiners, coroners and biological terrorism: a guidebook for surveillance and case management. Retrieved on October 23, 2009. Retrieved from http://www.cdc.gov/mmwr/preview/mmwrhtml/rr5308a1.htm

NYC.gov New York City Records. (2009). Photographs 1889 -1956, Retrieved on February 24, 2009, from http://www.nyc.gov/html/records/html/collections/collections_photographs.shtml

Office for Victims of Crime. (2008). First response to victims of crime: a guidebook for law enforcement officers. U.S. Department of Justice Office. Retrieved on April 14, 2009, from http://www.ojp.usdoj.gov/ovc/publications/infores/pdftxt/FirstResponseGuidebook.pdf

STAR Magazine (1994). O.J.'s statement to the LAPD. November 29, 1994. Retrieved on April 11, 2009, from http://www.law.umkc.edu/faculty/projects/ftrials/Simpson/OJSstmnt.html

Turvey, Brent E. (2008). Criminal Profiling: An introduction to behavioral evidence analysis 3rd Edition, Elsevier, Burlington, MA

United States Constitution. (1787).

USDOJ (2006). Criminal victimization in the United States. Retrieved on March 10, 2009, from http://www.ojp.usdoj.gov/bjs/pub/pdf/cvus/current/cv0633.pdf

USlaw.com (2009). Retrieved on October 20, 2009. Retrieved from http://www.uslaw.com/us_law_dictionary/c/Circumstantial+Evidence

United States Fire Administration (2001). Arson in the United States. Retrieved on June 24, 2009, from http://www.usfa.dhs.gov/downloads/pdf/tfrs/v1i8-508.pdf

YouTube (2006). Clinton, I did not have sexual relations with that woman... Retrieved on April 9, 2009, from http://www.youtube.com/watch?v=KiIP_KDQmXs posted on August 30, 2006.

Wyatt, K. (2008). Anonymous rape tests are going nationwide. Associated Press. Retrieved on April 10, 2009, from http://abcnews.go.com/Health/Story?id=4847901&page=1

Zulawski, D. E., Wicklander, D. (2001). Practical aspects of interview & interrogation: 2nd Edition. Boca Raton, Fl: CRC Press

Court Cases Cited

Aguilar v. Texas 378 US 108 (1964)

Arizona v. Grant 143 p.3d 379 (2006)

Brady v. Maryland 373 U.S. 83 (1963)

California v. Greenwood 486 U.S. 35 (1988)

Carroll v. The United States 267 U.S. 132 (1925)

Chimel v. California 395 U.S. 752 (1969)

Coolidge v. New Hampshire 403 U.S. 443

Daubert v. Merrell Dow Pharmaceuticals, Inc. 507 US 904 (1993)

Flippo v. West Virginia 528 U.S. 11 (1999)

Frazier v. Cupp 394 U.S. 731 (1969)

Frye v. United States 293 F. 1013 (1923)

Grant v. City of Long Beach 315 F. 3d 1081 (2002)

Illinois v. Caballes 543 U.S. 455 (2005)

Illinois v. Gates 462 US 213 (1983)

Kirby v. Illinois 406 US 682 (1972)

Maryland v. Buie 494 U.S. 325 (1990)

Mapp v. Ohio 367 U.S. 643 (1961)

Mincey v. Arizona 437 U.S. 385 (1978)

Miranda v. Arizona 384 U.S. 436 (1966)

New York v. Quarles 467 US 649 (1984)

People v. DeBour 40 NY 2d. 210 (1976)

People v. Johnson 81 NY 2d 828 (1993)

People v. LeGrand 8 N.Y.3d 449 (2007)

People v. Mitchell 39 NY2d 173 (1976)

People v. Rosario 9 NY2d. 286 (1961)

Sheriff v. Bessey 914 P.2d 618 (Nevada 1996)

South Dakota v. Opperman 428 U.S. 364 (1976)

Spinelli v. the United States 393 US 410 (1969)

State v. Cayward 552 S.2d 971 (Florida 1989)

Stovall v. Denno 388 U.S. 293 (1967)

Tennison v. San Francisco, No. 06-15426

Terry v. Ohio 392 U.S. 1 (1968)

Thompson v. Louisiana 469 U.S. 17 (1984)

United States v. Crews 445 U.S. 463 (1980)

United States v. Wade 388 US 218 (1967)

Weeks v. The United States 232 U.S. 383 (1914)

Index